ALMANAC
OF THE
GROSS,
DISGUSTING
& TOTALLY
REPULSIVE

A Compendium
of Fulsome Facts

By Eric Elfman

Illustrations by Ginny Pruitt

RANDOM HOUSE NEW YORK

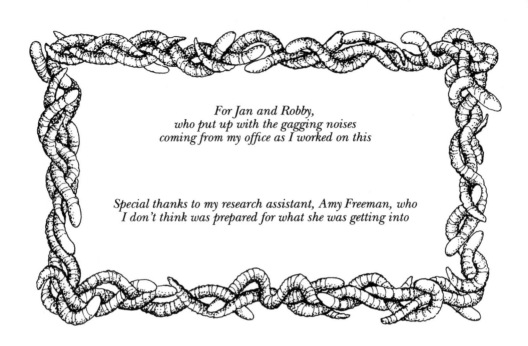

For Jan and Robby,
who put up with the gagging noises
coming from my office as I worked on this

Special thanks to my research assistant, Amy Freeman, who
I don't think was prepared for what she was getting into

Cover illustration: Marcela Cabrera
Page layout by Frank Loose Design, Portland, Oregon

Library of Congress Cataloging-in-Publication Data

Elfman, Eric.
Almanac of the gross, disgusting & totally repulsive: a compendium of
fulsome facts/ written by Eric Elfman; illustrations by Ginny Pruitt.
    p. cm.
Includes index.
ISBN 0-679-85805-9 (pbk.)
1. Almanacs, Children's. [1. Almanacs.] I. Pruitt, Ginny, ill.
II. Title.
AY81.J8E42 1994
031.02—dc20   93-48678

Manufactured in the United States of America   10 9 8 7 6 5 4 3 2 1

CONTENTS

INTRODUCTION

Why do we enjoy things that are gross?

Surely there is no pleasure in stepping into a pile of dog poop. Nobody enjoys biting into an apple and finding a worm. We don't go out of our way to get athlete's foot, eat moldy bread, or smell bad breath.

And yet, on some level, at some safe distance, we do like things that are gross. Why else would you be reading this book?

There is something about disgustingness that people enjoy and seek out. Some common thread that makes us laugh at the nauseating things that happen to others. Psychoanalysts believe that we enjoy gross things because we haven't outgrown a stage from our infancy—when things like a wet, warm diaper were all we knew and loved.

In any case, for whatever reason, fascination with things gross has always been with us. Gross entertainment, which so many people find fault with today, is not unique to the 20th century. As far back as the 1300s, Geoffrey Chaucer, in *The Canterbury Tales,* one of the foremost works of English literature, used gross bodily functions— defecation, flatulence, urination, etc.—to animate his characters. Today, scholars spend their lives studying Chaucer's work. Does that mean college professors years from now will be lecturing their students about the subtleties of Beavis and Butthead? Only time will tell...

WARNING!

This book may make you sick. For your convenience, "Barf Bag" warnings have been added to warn you when you are approaching information that is particularly vile.

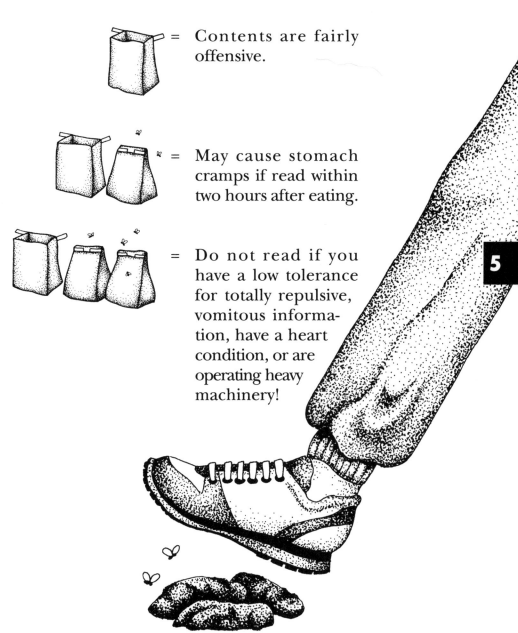

= Contents are fairly offensive.

= May cause stomach cramps if read within two hours after eating.

= Do not read if you have a low tolerance for totally repulsive, vomitous information, have a heart condition, or are operating heavy machinery!

5

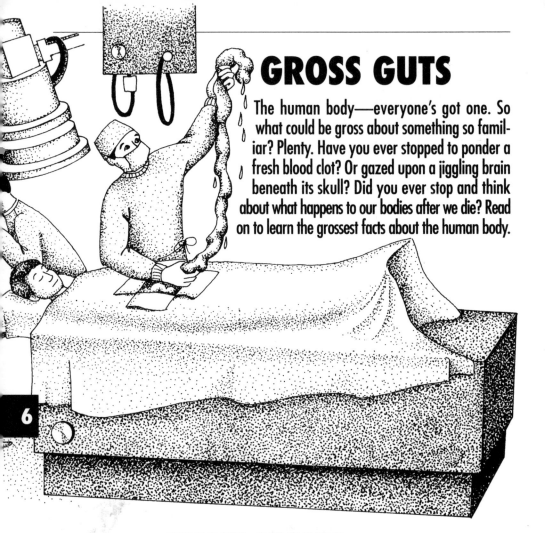

GROSS GUTS

The human body—everyone's got one. So what could be gross about something so familiar? Plenty. Have you ever stopped to ponder a fresh blood clot? Or gazed upon a jiggling brain beneath its skull? Did you ever stop and think about what happens to our bodies after we die? Read on to learn the grossest facts about the human body.

ODIOUS ORGANS

Body parts. Some can be very pretty. Some are not. But even the most benign ones can become totally gross when something goes wrong with them!

THE BRAIN

Made mostly of water, your brain is a mushy soft, pink-brown mass that weighs in at about three pounds. The surface is grooved and looks a little like a walnut. If something goes wrong with a person's brain, a special doctor called a neurosurgeon may operate on it.

Brain surgery is usually performed with the patient awake. Because the brain has no nerve endings, the patient does not feel pain while the doctor probes around inside his or her head. But the most strenuous part of the surgery is getting *to* the brain in the first place. First the surgeon uses a scalpel to cut open a flap of skin in the scalp. (Patients *are* given a local anesthetic to endure this hair-raising part of the procedure.) The doctor then drills a hole in the skull with a special power drill. Next he uses a sterile handsaw to cut a hole in the skull. (This piece of skull is removed, wrapped in gauze, and kept nearby on the instrument table.) Finally, the doctor cuts through a tough membrane around the brain, called the *dura mater,* and folds it over, exposing the brain.

7

Boxing and the Brain

In 1965, Dr. Milton Helpern, New York City's chief medical examiner, performed autopsies on boxers who died after they had been knocked out in the ring. Dr. Helpern was shocked by the effect of the numerous violent blows to the head that the boxers endured. Unlike normal, uninjured brains, which are solid masses of gray matter, the brains he was examining were actually *liquefied.* Helpern wrote in *Medical World News* that when holes were drilled in the heads of the dead boxers, "brain tissue oozed out like toothpaste from a tube."

THE NOSE

Our ability to smell comes from two yellow-brown patches of cells deep inside the nose. On these cells, tiny hairlike receptors called *dendrites* lie submerged under a thin layer of mucus. As we inhale, we breathe in molecules in the air, which get absorbed into this mucus layer and touch the dendrites. The dendrites then send signals to the brain, which translates these signals into the smells we perceive.

Nobody Nose the Trouble I've Seen

Sitting as it does in the center of your face, your nose is exposed to every kind of adverse condition you encounter, making it prone to all sorts of troubles. A doctor who specializes in nose, ear, and throat ailments is called an otolaryngologist (oh-toh-LAYR-in-gahl-oh-jist). Some of the things a nose doctor must contend with are:

Rhinitis. In this condition, the mucus in the nose becomes thick and swimming with bacteria. The mucus putrefies (or rots), and dries into a yellow, green, or black crust. The nose, instead of smelling other things, begins *itself* to stink!

Rhinitis caseosa. In this case, the nose fills with a horrible-smelling, cheesy material, which is actually pus rotting in the nasal cavity. In a bad case, there may be more than three inches of the gunk backed up inside the nose. To get it out, the doctor sometimes has to insert a bent probe into the nose and poke at the mass to break it into smaller, cheesy chunks so it can then be removed.

Objects in the nose. Small children often stick anything they can get their hands on into their nose, including screws, buttons, hooks, beans, and more. If the object becomes stuck in the nose, a doctor will insert a probe up the nasal cavity to determine the object's size, shape, and location. Objects can then be removed with tweezers or through surgery. If an object remains in the nose long enough, calcium and other minerals in the nose form a crust around the object, making it more difficult to remove.

Maggots in the nose. This is mostly a problem in India, South America, and other tropical countries, where flies sometimes lay their eggs in a person's nose. Soon the person begins to feel a tickling in his or her nose, followed by the hair-raising realization that *something is alive inside their nose.* The afflicted person then begins sneezing out a thick, foul-smelling, bloody discharge, filled with maggots. More than three hundred maggots may be in the victim's nose, eating and destroying the mucous membrane and cartilage. The victim's sinuses are filled with larvae, their excrement, and the tattered remains of rotting nasal tissue.

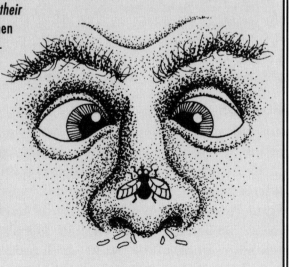

8

THE MOUTH

Have you ever stopped to think about how much you use your mouth every day? Chewing and swallowing, breathing, gnashing your teeth, and swishing your tongue about constantly, day in and day out. It would be a miracle if the occasional problem didn't befall such a busy orifice. The following are some of the most disgusting problems the mouth is prone to.

Bad Breath: People have been offended by bad breath for centuries. In the mid-1800s, a book entitled *The Toilet in Ancient and Modern Times* advised that "stinking breath" was caused either by rotten teeth, a diseased stomach, or worms. Today we know that bad breath is brought on by a variety of causes, most usually food we've eaten, or particles of food rotting in our mouths. Amazingly enough, you can also get strong garlic breath simply by coming into physical contact with a piece of garlic. (Say, if a clove touches your hand.)

One especially stinky type of bad breath that is caused by what we eat is *halitosis*. When fats in food are not properly broken down, they become a foul-smelling substance that the blood transports to the lungs, where it is exhaled in the breath—making the breath smell terrible.

Rotten Teeth: When a tooth dies, the pulpy mass of nerves and blood vessels at the center of the tooth begins to rot. Soon pus forms at the root of the tooth and begins to drain out through the mouth or nose. Until the tooth is removed, pus continues to form and drain. A root canal—a certain kind of dental operation—can sometimes save a tooth. The dentist opens the root and removes the dead pulp, then fills the cavity with a paste made of rubber, zinc oxide, barium sulfide, and resin.

TASTELESS TRIVIA:
The record for the largest calcified mass (a covering of calcium deposits) formed around a foreign object in a person's nose goes to a chunk the size of a hen's egg.

9

FOUL FACT:
Your mouth produces about 2½ pints of saliva a day—or almost two gallons of spit a week!

THE TONGUE

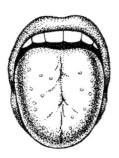

That long pink thing inside your mouth. Taste buds on the tongue allow us to taste what we eat. And the tongue itself helps us to swallow food and form words. Unfortunately, the tongue is subject to a number of "tasteless" problems. Listed below are a few of the worst.

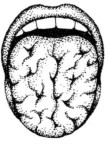

Coated Tongue: Once in a while, a slimy coat may appear on the tongue for no apparent reason, while a dry, powdery coat of organic matter may occur due to an infection.

Fissured Tongue: A deep crack or fold appears in the tongue. It is a common condition among people with larger than average tongues. There is nothing wrong with it and it doesn't hurt—however, particles of food may collect at the bottom of the crack and rot, causing a burning sensation.

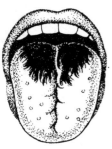

Hairy Tongue: The tongue is covered by a thick coating of what looks like white, yellowish, brown, or black hair. (The hair is actually a threadlike growth on the taste buds.) Although harmless (it sometimes occurs after having a fever, taking antibiotics, or overusing mouthwash), it looks very bizarre.

THE APPENDIX

A wormlike tube that extends from the large intestine, the appendix produces a stinking, greenish yellow, functionless fluid. If the appendix becomes infected (a condition called appendicitis), it fills with pus. This pus mixes with the appendix's own natural fluids, forming a lethal combination. If the swollen appendix bursts, its infected, putrid contents will pour into the body, and if untreated, cause death.

THE HEART

This meaty double pump spews out two thousand gallons of blood a day. Oddly enough, the heart doesn't need a body to pump. As long as it is kept warm and supplied with oxygen, the heart will continue to beat even if it is removed from the chest. Experiments have shown that even a small *piece* of tissue cut from the heart will continue to contract and expand for a brief time.

You Gotta Have Heart

The ancient Aztecs practiced human sacrifice, believing that their sun god needed human blood to survive—such vast quantities of blood, in fact, that finding sacrificial victims became the main reason the Aztec Empire kept expanding its territory.

The only acceptable sacrifice to the sun god was the human heart. The victim was painted with red and white stripes, and a black circle was drawn around his or her mouth. The victim was marched up the steps of the temple, then thrown backward over the stone altar. Four priests held down the prisoner's arms and legs, and a fifth pressed down his or her neck. The high priest cut open the chest of the fully conscious human offering with the *tecpatl,* a special knife used for the ritual. Then, reaching into the opening, the priest yanked out the still-beating heart and held it up to the sun.

Some anthropologists estimate that the Aztecs sacrificed up to twenty thousand people a year this way!

11

THE BLADDER

A holding tank for urine, the bladder has walls that expand like an accordion as it fills, drip by drip, with liquid waste. As the bladder fills, pressure rises, creating the desire to urinate. You can hold off going to the bathroom until the pressure inside the bladder becomes too great—usually when about a pint of urine has been stored. A bladder filled with a pint of urine forms a ball about four inches in diameter, approximately the size of a softball.

THE COLON

After the small intestine absorbs all the nutrients from the food you eat, the remaining semiliquid material is passed on to the colon, or large intestine. As this wet waste travels down the three-foot long colon, its lining absorbs most of the water back into the body. The remaining solid waste then travels into the rectum, where it is expelled through the anus.

SKIN ERUPTIONS AND DISRUPTIONS

You may have heard that beauty is skin deep. Well, you don't have to look any deeper than the skin to find a lot that's pretty gross to look at!

ACNE

Acne is a skin disorder that is caused by an infection or blockage of the hair follicles, resulting in blemishes called blackheads and pimples. There are two or more oil glands for every hair on your body. Under normal conditions, the cells around these glands fill with fatty material and burst open, pouring oil onto the hair and skin and keeping them lubricated.

When these glands produce too much oil, however, the pore openings become blocked with old, dried grease and trapped particles of dirt, forming a blemish. A blackhead is a blemish with a tiny black "head." The black in a blackhead is from skin pigment that darkens when exposed to the air. The long, yellowish tendril that can be squeezed out of a blackhead is the dried grease from the gland. Whiteheads, on the other hand, are caused when one of these blocked pores is so packed with bacteria and gunk that no air can enter. White blood cells fight off the bacteria, filling the pimple with pus.

TASTELESS TRIVIA:
Natural casings for sausages are made from the intestines of sheep, pigs, and oxen. And, yes, intestines in these animals serve the same function as they do in people— to transport food through the body while reducing it to feces.

12

In serious cases of acne, seriously large pimples, called sebaceous cysts (see-BAY-shus sists), sometimes form. They may be up to an inch in diameter. Skin doctors, called dermatologists, use large needles to pop these gargantuan zits. (Don't do this at home—popping pimples can result in pitted skin and infections.) In a very severe form of acne called acne conglobata, the cysts form close together, producing boggy and dead areas of skin. In this condition, the cysts are constantly discharging their pus, forming a crust over the deep, dead depression in the flesh.

ATHLETE'S FOOT

Caused by a fungus that enjoys warm, moist areas, a case of athlete's foot may last for years. It can cause painful cracks and blisters between the toes, and raw areas and scales on the rest of the foot. The fungus can live anywhere bare feet may go—on rugs, hardwood floors, in shoes. Sometimes the fungus even hides under one of the sufferer's own toenails. A person may then treat his or her athlete's foot, and watch it seem to clear up, only to have the fungus under the nail reinfect the foot.

13

BOILS

Boils are large areas of the skin that, because of invading bacteria, become swollen with pus and eventually burst. In extreme cases, the boils become carbuncles, a series of interconnected boils. When this type of boil comes to a head and pops, it not only discharges the pus-filled fluid, but the skin falls off the affected area, and a deep open sore results.

SCABIES

Scabies, an itchy skin condition, is caused by a tiny insect called a mite, which digs tunnels under the skin (often between the fingers), where it lays its eggs. The tunnels then become infected and fill with pus. When the eggs hatch, the larvae gather around the hair follicles on top of the skin, where they grow into mature mites. Then they may spread to another person.

WASTE 101

It is often said that what goes up must come down. Less often said, but equally true, is what goes in must come out ...

FLUID WASTE

The average person loses about five pints of liquid a day, in the following ways:

14

Urine 2.5 pints

Perspiration 1.25 pints

Exhaled moisture from lungs 1 pint

Feces (about three-fourths of fecal matter is water) .25 pint

Perspiration

With more than two million sweat glands in our bodies, we produce more than a pint of sweat every day (and even more when we exercise). Butyric acid (the smelly substance in rancid butter) and hydrogen sulfide (the material that puts the stench in rotten eggs) are two chemicals found in our sweat that make it stink. To make us even smellier, the bacteria that live on our skin swim in our sweat, eat the nutrients they find there, and release a potent-smelling ammonia waste.

> ## Caution: Bathing May Be Hazardous to Your Health
> As late as the mid-1700s, doctors and philosophers warned against bathing. At the time, our "animal odors" were considered a very important and socially respectable part of our bodies. A strong smell was believed to show how vigorous and alive you were, and the worse you smelled, the more attractive you were thought to be.

Urine

Fresh urine is odorless and nearly free of bacteria—it has even been used as a disinfectant in emergencies, such as in battlefield situations. The pungent smell of old, stale urine comes from bacteria that have had time to grow in the urine and decompose the urea found naturally in urine, turning it to ammonia.

If you urinate and hair comes out with your urine, you may have a condition known as a dermatoid cyst in your bladder. These cysts can contain hair, swallowed teeth, and solids that have been calcified. In another painful bladder condition, called Hunner's ulcer, the urine may contain blood, pus, mucus, and/or mineral particles.

SOLID WASTE

Every bite of food you take, every morsel you consume, contains material that your body won't digest—and it has to come out one way or another...

Feces

After its long journey through your intestine, feces (FEE-sees) emerge from the anus. Almost a *third* of the solid matter in feces is bacteria from inside your intestine. Some of these bacteria are dead, but the rest are still alive. They group in colonies and feed on the cells, mucus, and tiny bits of indigestible food that make up the solid fecal matter.

FOUL FACT:

15

The most pungent-smelling feces comes from eating meat, slightly less rank waste comes from eating vegetables, and the least aromatic variety results from a diet rich in dairy products.

Diarrhea

Diarrhea is feces that is watered down because it has passed through the large intestine too quickly for the water to be removed. Diarrhea may occur because the intestine is irritated by food that can't be digested, because of a bacterial infection, or due to a nervous condition. When there is an infection in the digestive system, diarrhea may also contain mucus, pus, or blood.

GAS

Flatulence

Flatus (FLAY-tus) is the technical term for "passing wind." It is a combination of swallowed air and fermented gases produced by the bacteria living in our intestines.

So why does gas smell? Because very tiny amounts of some very stinky substances—ammonia, hydrogen sulfide, indole, skatole, volatile amines, and volatile fatty acids—are also present.

TASTELESS TRIVIA:
Every day, the average person passes about half a quart of gas. It is normal to pass gas anywhere from ten to fifteen times a day.

16

Go out with a Bang!
When hydrogen and methane (two gases normally present in the intestine) are combined in the right proportion with oxygen, you have the ingredients for an explosion. There have been recorded cases, from years ago, where surgeons opened up a patient's intestines for an operation at the same time a piece of equipment emitted a spark, resulting in the patient *exploding* on the operating table!

Eructation

Eructation (ih-ruck-TAY-shun), also known as burping or belching, occurs when gas from the stomach escapes through the mouth. Although in some cultures belching after a meal is considered a compliment, passing gas from the opposite end of the alimentary canal is considered socially unacceptable everywhere—especially at the dinner table!

MUCUS

The clear, thick, slimy liquid called mucus that lines our nose, mouth, throat, lungs, urinary system, and digestive tract protects our internal organs by coating the nearly twenty billion particles of pollution, dust, dirt, and chemicals that we inhale every day.

Mucus is produced by the mucous membrane, the smooth, wet, reddish orange lining of the digestive tract, lungs, and urinary system. Cilia, tiny hairlike structures, cover the entire mucous membrane. Moving quickly in rhythm, cilia keep our mucus zipping along at about five millimeters a minute. Working like a microscopic escalator, the cilia move the mucus up and out of the lungs to the throat, where the mucus can then be swallowed, coughed up, or spat out.

17

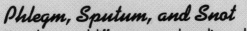
Phlegm, Sputum, and Snot

Mucus has several different names, depending on how one disposes of it. Coughing is often an impulse to remove phlegm—thick mucus full of foreign particles that collects in the throat. When phlegm is spat out instead of swallowed, it is called sputum—a mixture of mucus, particles, and saliva.

Snot, mucus that coats foreign particles trapped in the nose hairs, is removed when you blow (or pick) your nose.

PUS

When bacteria or other foreign particles invade our body, our white blood cells, also called leukocytes (LOO-kuh-sites), counterattack. White blood cells crawl along the insides of our blood vessels, almost like separate one-celled organisms living within our bodies. They wrap themselves around the invading organisms and eat them. Millions of white blood cells die in this battle, and the thick, gooey, white liquid called pus is made up of the corpses of these dead white blood cell soldiers.

VOMIT

During normal vomiting, your abdominal wall and diaphragm slowly squeeze together, tightening on the stomach between them like a pair of pliers clamping down on a sausage. Your esophagus opens and the watery, partially digested food is squeezed out of your stomach, up your throat, and out of your mouth.

Another type of vomiting is called (for good reason), projectile vomiting. When you projectile-vomit, the muscles of the stomach itself clench together forcefully, shooting the food up the throat and out through the mouth in a powerful spray. (Think of Linda Blair in *The Exorcist,* vomiting pea soup.)

18

TASTELESS TRIVIA:
How Do YOU Say "Throw Up?"
- Barf
- Puke
- Upchuck
- Lose your lunch
- Hurl
- Toss your cookies
- Blow chunks
- Worship the porcelain god
- Spew

GERMS AND WORMS

Our bodies are like traveling luxury hotels, each of us playing unwitting host to billions of nearly invisible creatures. That's right, each of us is crawling with germs and other creatures, inside and out—and there's not a thing we can do about most of them.

MAKING YOUR SKIN CRAWL

Right now, uncountable millions of bacteria are crawling around on our bodies. They are everywhere on our skin and hair. They reproduce, eat, and leave waste on us day and night. Wars rage, literally right under our noses, as different species of bacteria battle each other to the death.

Unfortunately, you can't get rid of them by washing. Oh, you can scrub your face clean of bacteria temporarily, but they come back almost instantly—and often in greater numbers than before!

And just how many microbes are living on you? Huge populations. On your forehead alone, there are over eight million per square inch! There may be as many as one and a half million just on the tip of your nose. (If bacteria were people, that would be the population of Philadelphia!)

These sound like great numbers, but in fact bacteria are so tiny that thirty million of them pressed together could fit on the period at the end of this sentence.

MITES IN OUR EYES

Bacteria aren't the only living things that make their homes in and on our bodies. Tiny creatures related to spiders, called follicle mites, were first discovered living in the holes at the base of our eyelashes in 1972. They spend their entire lives mating, eating, and relieving themselves among

19

our lashes. A favorite food of the follicle mite is eyeliner. It contains nearly all of the nutrients they need to survive.

GERMS IN OUR GUTS

So you think there are a lot of bacteria on the outside of your body? Well, those figures are nothing compared to the number of them living inside your digestive tract! In fact, it has been estimated that there may be up to a hundred trillion bacteria in just $\frac{1}{30}$ of an ounce of feces. (If bacteria were people, that would be two thousand times the population living on Earth!) They live mainly inside your large intestine, feeding on the remains of hard-to-digest foods, such as beans. Their waste product is a gas that comes out of us when we pass wind.

THE WORMS CRAWL IN

Wherever human waste is not disposed of properly, parasitic worms—worms that, well, *worm* their way into your body to feed—are a danger. The eggs of these parasites are found in the feces and sometimes in the urine of people who carry the adult worms inside them. When this human waste gets onto crops or food that animals feed on, it gets into the animals' bloodstreams. When people then eat the contaminated animals, the cycle begins anew. Following are some of the most common parasites.

Flukes

Flukes are flat worms that spend most of their lives living inside humans. They are transmitted through human excrement or urine. When fluke-infested waste gets into a lake or pond, the eggs of the flukes hatch and the babies attach themselves to crabs, snails, or underwater vegetation. If you go for a swim or even just dip your feet in the infested water, the unimaginably thin flukes worm their way through your skin and into your body. Once inside, the worms swim to your liver, where they lay millions of eggs. Upon hatching, the millions of worms begin swimming around inside your veins, where they can live, if untreated, for up to twenty years. Some kinds of flukes cause few, if any, outward symptoms in their human hosts. Others can cause dysentery (an infectious disease of the large intestine that causes violent bloody diarrhea), abdominal pain, and miscellaneous other uncomfortable conditions.

Tapeworms

Tapeworms are long, flat worms that can live in people's intestines. Using hooks and a sucker on its head, the worm attaches itself to the inside of the small intestine. As it feeds, the tapeworm grows a series of flat segments filled with eggs—up to several thousand eggs a day! These flat segments, which resemble a piece of tape, may stretch for thirty feet through your intestines. As the tape gets longer, the end breaks off and is passed out of the body along with the feces. When cows and pigs eat grain contaminated by human feces that contain tapeworm eggs, they become carriers themselves. When meat from these contaminated animals is undercooked, the person who eats it will soon have a tapeworm inside him or her.

Ascarides (a-SKAR-ih-deez)

After hatching in your small intestine, ascarid worms hitch a ride in your bloodstream to your lungs, where they develop through the early stages of their lives. When nearly full-

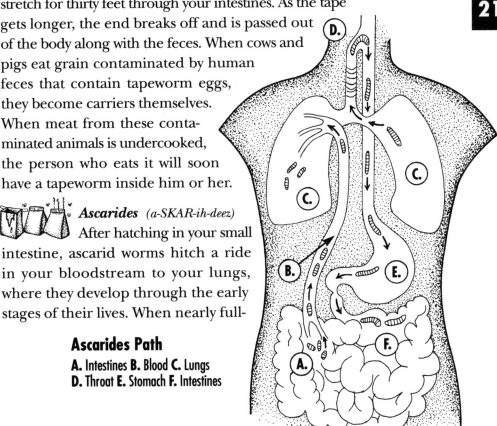

Ascarides Path
A. Intestines B. Blood C. Lungs
D. Throat E. Stomach F. Intestines

21

grown, the worms, which look like small earthworms, crawl up your windpipe to your throat, where they are swallowed. They then travel through your stomach and into your intestines, where they remain for the rest of their lives.

Although a person with ascarid worms living inside him or her may suffer a fever and experience some coughing as the larvae pass through his or her lungs, the adult worms generally cause no ill health effects. They are usually detected by the presence of their eggs in a host's feces, although adult worms can sometimes be seen crawling around in the host's feces, vomit, or sputum.

22

Hookworms

Hookworms are curved little worms about half an inch long that live in soil that has been contaminated by human feces. When you walk on contaminated ground with bare feet, the worms bore their way through the bottoms of your feet. The worms then reproduce in your body, and hundreds, perhaps thousands, of the creatures attach themselves to your small intestine with their sharp teeth while they suck your blood. This can cause your hair to change color and texture and cause your fingernails to become flat, or even to cave in.

Pinworms

Children are the primary sufferers of pinworms—tiny, white, curly worms that make their home in the colon. After the worms mate in the colon, the pregnant female inches her way down to and out of the anus to lay her eggs under the skin folds around the edge of the anus. These eggs are spread by little children's fingers—they scratch at the eggs when the area becomes itchy, and then touch clothes, sheets, toys, doorknobs, anything they can reach. The eggs are so light they may even end up floating in the air. When little children put

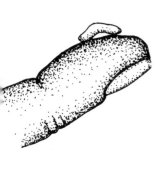

their fingers in their mouths, they swallow the eggs, which hatch in the intestine, and the worms make their way to the colon, where the whole cycle begins again.

SICKENING SENSES

Your senses allow you to experience the beauty of the world, both natural and man-made. Unfortunately, you can't turn your senses on and off. Sure, you can take off your eyeglasses or plug up your ears. But there is little you can do to keep odious odors, foul sounds, and terrible tastes from occasionally grossing you out.

23

SMELLIEST SMELLS

Ah, the advantages of modern life. From fresh meat and dairy products to water and sludge treatment plants, these niceties of the 20th century come with a price.

How would you like it if your home were downwind from an asphalt-processing plant or a slaughterhouse? According to one survey of complaints from the mid-1970s, the following is a list of the smelliest, stinkiest, most nauseating places to live near. As you read on, imagine what odors must emanate from them!

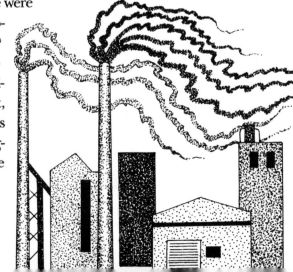

1. An asphalt-processing plant
2. A commercial waste incinerator
3. A wastewater treatment plant
4. A pig farm
5. A paint and varnish plant
6. A composting site
7. An iron foundry
8. A landfill
9. A slaughterhouse
10. A poultry farm
11. A fish-and-meat processing plant
12. A sludge-treatment plant

Paris in the Springtime—Phooey!

Despite the many disgusting odors we must contend with today, most people living in the 20th century have it pretty easy, smell-wise. In the past, even royalty had to regularly breathe smells worse than you will probably ever know. For instance, Paris, in 1740, was the center of science, art, fashion, and taste, but it was also, said Louis Sebastien Mercier, a French playwright of the time, "the center of stench." According to Jean-Jacques Rousseau, an 18th-century French philosopher, in the courthouse, in the museum, at the opera, even at the palace of Versailles, "one does not know where to sit in summer, without inhaling the odor of stagnant urine." Courtyards, corridors, and alleys were full of urine and feces. And regarding the main street, Mercier says it was "covered with stagnant water and dead cats."

NASTIEST NOISES

Some people can't stand the sound of fingernails scraping down a blackboard. Others become nearly sick if someone lets air screech out of the pinched neck of a balloon. Just thinking about these sounds make some people uncomfortable.

Why do some sounds affect us so? To find out, test subjects were exposed to extremely loud, intense industrial grinding for long periods of time. Their reactions:

1. Gagging
2. Vibration in the eyes
3. Ear pain
4. Nausea
5. Giddiness
6. Severe coughing
7. Sore throat
8. Body aches
9. Extreme fatigue

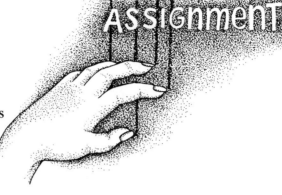

Why do our bodies respond in such ways? Scientists speculate that in ancient times our ancestors had to be able to react instantly and fight or run away from loud noises, because such sounds almost always signaled danger.

Today, when people are exposed to loud noises, their bodies respond in the same ways. When the noise is continuous, however, their bodies stay in the fight or flight reaction for the duration of the sound. This extended muscle tenseness all over the body causes the gross effects listed above.

TASTELESS TASTES

Surveys are constantly being performed to find out how different foods taste to different people, what they like, and what they don't like.

According to surveyed consumers, the most undesirably flavored pork products come from uncastrated male pigs. When heated, the flavor of the fat in these products is described as "urinelike." Another horrid taste comes from meat products that are irradiated, that is, subjected to radiation to kill bacteria and preserve the meat. People report that irradiated meat tastes "like a wet dog smells!"

25

DEATH BECOMES YOU

Death. The final frontier. The last unknown. For centuries, philosophers and theologians have sought answers about what happens to us after we die. Of course, they are asking questions about the soul. As far as what happens to the body, well, we know the rank reality.

THE RIGORS OF RIGOR MORTIS

After a person dies, the temperature of the body gradually lowers. Blood settles because it is no longer circulating, causing the lowest parts of the body to appear red, while the places drained of blood appear nearly white.

Three to seven hours after death, the muscles in a dead body become stiff—a condition called *rigor mortis* (literally, the "stiffness of death"). When blood circulation stops, the lack of oxygen causes sugars in the muscles to break down to simpler forms, finally becoming lactic acid, a chemical that causes the muscles to stiffen. Rigor mortis starts in the face, beginning in the muscles of the lower jaw, then in the neck and eyelids. Police officers in search of clues at crime scenes sometimes have to break the stiffened fingers of murder victims to open their clenched fists. Rigor mortis lasts at full intensity about twelve hours, then slowly starts to disappear. Within forty-eight hours, a body is soft and flexible again.

DECOMPOSING—NEARLY EVERY BODY'S DOING IT!

The first sign of decomposition (decay) in a dead body is a green tinge on the skin over the belly about forty-eight hours after death. This is caused by the bacteria that live within the intestines beginning to eat the body from the inside out. (Scientists aren't exactly sure why these bacteria wait until we are dead before eating us.) The bacteria swarm like an army through

FOUL FACT:

Different body parts decompose at different rates. Nails become loosened from fingers and toes around the twentieth day. Eyes take about two months to rot. Brains, because they are protected by skulls, deteriorate very slowly. They are also far from the gut, where decomposition originates. Bones and teeth, of course, last the longest.

26

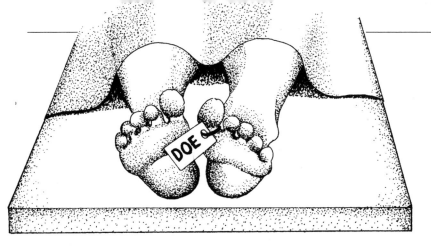

the intestines, chomping everything in sight. They then proceed to liquefy the body tissues.

When a corpse gets cold enough (below about 50 degrees), it stops rotting—which is why corpses are kept in refrigerators at mortuaries. An unembalmed, refrigerated body will stay fairly well preserved for three days.

EMBALMING

To keep a body from decomposing for as long as possible (even after it is buried), it is embalmed. This is a fairly simple process: as soon as the body arrives at the mortuary or funeral home, the undertaker makes a two-inch incision in the skin over a major artery in either the groin (although fatty tissue sometimes makes this a difficult place to reach), the base of the neck, or under the arm, and attaches a pump. Embalming fluid—a solution that kills bacteria and other microbes, slowing down the deterioration of the corpse—is pumped in, while blood is drained through a tube inserted in a vein opened in the same area as the pump. A mortician can tell when a body is finished because it feels stiffer.

The next step in the embalming process is to insert a vacuum tube into the abdomen. The tube sucks up all fecal matter, urine, and the undigested contents of the stomach. The now empty intestines, colon,

TASTELESS TRIVIA: You can induce a temporary, harmless lactic acid buildup in your own hand, to simulate a state approaching rigor mortis. Rapidly open and close your hand as long as you can. You will notice it becoming harder and harder to keep doing this—that's because lactic acid is forming in the muscles of your fingers and hand, stiffening them.

27

Ghastly Gas

Bacteria munching away at a corpse produce huge buildups of gas inside the body. These gases can swell a body up like a balloon.

Before bodies were kept refrigerated in mortuaries, undertakers found another way to prevent this bloating. They would prick tiny holes into a body and then briefly hold a candle to the openings. Long blue flames would appear, fed by the gases escaping from the corpse. These unearthly fires would remain lit for three or four days, until all the gas was gone.

---

bladder, and stomach are then also filled with embalming fluid.

Embalming is done almost routinely, but especially when a body is going to be viewed at a funeral. In some states, if a body is going to be transported aboard a bus, train, airplane, or other commercial vehicle (in the luggage compartment, of course), it must be embalmed for health and sanitation purposes.

BURIAL RITES THROUGHOUT THE WORLD

Throughout history, different peoples have treated human remains in a variety of ways. From eating dead bodies to trying to preserve them forever, human societies have responded to the mystery of death in a number of mind-boggling ways. Many (if not most) of these ancient practices have not been used for centuries. But as we know from the news, people (for widely different reasons) still commit cannibalism with some regularity. Who knows, but that in isolated pockets, remote villages, and suburban backyards, these and similar practices still continue?

Cannibalism: In many primitive societies around the world, from Australia to South America, it was once considered a proper and fitting show of respect to eat the dead.

On the islands of Indonesia, between Java and New Guinea, cannibalism was outlawed near the beginning of the 20th century. However, its practice as a sacred ritual in some villages continues today in secret. As a respected male elder of a tribe nears death, he is ritually killed by the other men of the tribe with a bamboo dagger. The body of the elder tribesman is then cooked and eaten by the tribe. His head, however, is removed before cooking, and the young men of the tribe eat the brain raw.

Jar Me: Up until about sixty years ago, dead bodies in Borneo were squeezed into jars that were kept in the house of the dead person's family for a year. A tube made from bamboo led from the bottom of the jar to the ground outside the house, allowing liquid to drain from the rotting body. When the year was over, what was left of the body was transferred to a smaller ceremonial vessel and buried with great rejoicing, and probably some relief.

Mummy Dearest: The ancient Egyptians believed in a physical life after death (as opposed to the idea of a purely spiritual afterlife), so they went to great lengths to preserve the dead bodies of royalty and the very rich in as lifelike a state as possible.

29

HOW MUMMIES WERE MADE

1. A priest would cut into the abdomen of a dead body and remove all the internal organs. (These would then be preserved separately in small jars.)
2. An iron hook was inserted up the nose and into the brain. The brain was then pulled out through the nostrils.
3. The now organless body was placed in a vat of salt and mineral water to dissolve the fatty tissue underneath the skin. The head was kept bobbing above the solution so it would not dissolve, the goal being to keep the facial features recogniz-

TASTELESS TRIVIA:
Because newborn infants have very few bacteria inside them, when they die they tend to mummify (become dried-up and preserved) instead of decompose.

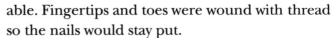

FOUL FACT:

The poor, who could not afford mummification, simply washed the body and then packed it in salt for seventy days. The body was stored in the home for quite some time, and taken out on special ceremonial occasions.

able. Fingertips and toes were wound with thread so the nails would stay put.

4. After soaking for seventy days, the body was removed from the vat and rinsed with fresh water. It was then packed with various preservatives, like the mineral natron, and resin, taken from plants. The skull was filled by injecting thick fluids through the nostrils, and the outside of the body was slathered with resin and fat. Finally, the mummified body was wrapped in linen.

Some mummies are still extremely well preserved. Their features are recognizable thousands of years after they died. In fact, scientists have been able to obtain DNA samples from the intact skin tissue of dead pharaohs.

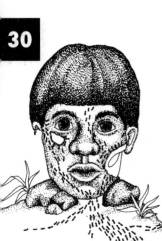

Hot off the Griddle: As recently as the 1930s, the Banziri tribe of central Africa placed their dead on a grid over a fire. The melting fat that dripped from the corpse was collected in pots, and mourners who gathered around the body rubbed this oil onto their hands and faces. They rinsed off the oil with warm water, and close relatives of the deceased would then drink this water.

Picked Clean and Painted Red: Until the turn of the century, natives of the Torres Strait Islands sawed the heads off their corpses and placed them over ant holes. After the heads were picked clean by the ants, the skulls would be painted red and set in fancy baskets.

Towers of Silence: Followers of the Zoroastrian religion, which was founded in Iran around the year 600 B.C., believe that earth, fire, and water are sacred elements that shouldn't be desecrated by death. Therefore human remains cannot be buried, cremated, or disposed of at sea. Instead, the Zoroastrians place their dead in tall stone towers open to the sky, called Towers of Silence, so that vultures can eat the corpses.

Today in Bombay, India, members of the Parsi community of Zoroastrians have seven such Towers of Silence. Unfortunately, many neighbors of the Parsi (some of whom live in luxurious apartment buildings) aren't members of the same religion, and their views are marred by the vultures eating corpses within the towers.

PREMATURE BURIAL

Before the invention of modern brain and heart monitoring devices to accurately measure brain and bodily activity, people were sometimes buried before they had actually died. There was so much concern about this that a Society for the Prevention of Premature Burial in America and England existed in 1911, and a magazine entitled *The Perils of Premature Burial* was published from 1906 to 1914. Suggestions to avoid burying people before they were dead were made, and carried out, such as tying a string around the finger of a corpse with the other end attached to a bell so that a person who wasn't quite dead could easily alert those around him or her.

One typical case of premature burial occurred in the early 1900s, involving George Hefdecker, a farmer in Erie, Pennsylvania. When George died, his family couldn't afford a cemetery plot or a proper funeral, so he was temporarily buried in a neighbor's plot in a plain wooden box. When his kin had scraped together enough money for a funeral, plot, and new casket, George's temporary coffin was dug up. The box was opened—and they found the now indisputably dead George with a grimace of horror upon his face. His hands and face were skinned and bloody, unmistakable signs that he had tried to claw his way out of the box.

EXHUMATION

The reverse of burial is exhumation, digging *out* of the earth. Occasionally, in the case of a mysterious death or to honor a person's memory by moving their corpse

31

to a more suitable final resting place, a dead body must be exhumed from its grave.

This is an unpleasant job, as a body will usually be partly or totally decomposed. When airtight coffin linings are opened, the people opening them must hold their breath or they can be overcome by gases produced during the process of decomposition.

For reasons scientists don't fully understand, bodies decompose at different rates. This was illustrated vividly by a case that occurred nearly a hundred years ago. A number of soldiers were buried together in a mass grave on a battlefield. Five years later, when they were dug up to be moved to a veterans' cemetery, it was discovered that, as one witness wrote, "some of them were skeletons, clothed with the remains of their belts, while others were still in such a state of preservation that their features could be recognized."

 ## TO ROT OR NOT TO ROT: ALTERNATIVES TO BURIAL

There's more to do with a dead body than just bury it. Consider the following choices that you can make about how to dispose of your mortal remains.

Organ harvesting: If you sign an agreement before you die, and if your body is intact and healthy, your organs can be used to help keep other people alive. If you are brought to a hospital near death, and the doctors don't believe they can save you, the people who are going to receive organs are notified to begin getting ready for their operations. (A heart and a pair of lungs are only good for a couple of hours after death.) When you finally die, the organ harvesters, special doctors who remove usable organs from dead bodies, come in and pick your body clean—kidneys, eyes, and anything else remotely useful are taken.

 ***Donating body to science:*** Some people get satisfaction from the knowledge that their death may help to advance scientific knowledge, and so they donate their whole bodies to medical schools or teaching hospitals to be used for research purposes. Every institution has its own unique procedure for accepting bodies, so institutions must be contacted individually to learn the steps required for donating your body to them.

Cremation: Many people choose to have their bodies cremated, or burned to ashes, after they die.

Consuming chambers, the ovens in which bodies are cremated, are built to withstand temperatures as high as 2,500 degrees Fahrenheit. The chamber's interior is a smooth and polished white. Fire never enters this chamber—it stays outside, circulating around it. When a body is placed in the chamber, the air inside is superheated and becomes a blinding white, and the body is incinerated. This takes about an hour and a half for the average body, reducing it to about five to seven pounds of ash. Depending on the laws of the state where the cremation took place, the ashes can then be buried, placed in an urn, or scattered on land or at sea.

Cryonics: The opposite of cremation, cryonics involves freezing the body immediately after death. This is done in the hope that future doctors will have the means to revive the body and cure the disease or condition that caused it to die. An economic alternative to preserving an entire body is to save only the head, cutting it off at the neck and freezing it in a vat of liquid nitrogen. People who do this hope that the technology will someday exist to reattach these heads to human or robotic bodies.

33

TASTELESS TRIVIA:
Urban legend has it that Walt Disney had his body cryonically preserved. This is untrue. In fact, Disney was cremated and is buried at Forest Lawn Cemetery in California.

NAUSEATING NATURE

Everywhere you look there is something gross to be found. But surely, you think, there is nothing repulsive in your neat, clean home. And positively *not* in the beauty of nature! Well . . . think again. Your dog, your shoes, your backyard, in fact, every room of your home is crawling with disgustingness. Read on, but be warned—you may never feel quite so comfortable anywhere, ever again.

SLIMIES

Slimy molds and fungi are *every*where, on *every*thing. Individually, they are so tiny they're invisible to the naked eye. But molds and fungi are slowly digesting everything in sight—the chair you're sitting in, the books on your shelves, your leather backpack, you name it.

FUNGI AND MOLD

The air is always filled with invisible spores, the reproductive cells of molds and fungi. Every second you are being assaulted by many different kinds of fungi. They are on you right now. Living and breeding. They're in the beams supporting your home, your breakfast cereal, and the paint on your walls. Skeptical? Leave a slice of bread on your counter for a couple of days. Where do you think that mold comes from? Even if the bread stays in your refrigerator for too long, it will get moldy.

The fungus rhizopus grows so quickly that a slice of bread or a banana will soon become black with it. One single rhizopus spore can grow to hundreds of millions of spores in a few days. Rhizopus is in every yard, farm, and forest, turning dead things into moldy dead things. It covers the earth. And rhizopus is only one of the *thousands* of different fungi in your home.

Of course, rotting and decay are necessary, and some might say beautiful, parts of nature. In converting dead plants and animals into fertile soil, fungi provide food for the next generation of plants, animals— and fungi!

Fungi Food

Fungi are saprophytes, which literally means "rotten plants." They are scavengers, living on dead material that they consume. Almost everything that is now alive (including you) will end up as fungi food. About the only things fungi don't eat are metals. Fungi can eat plastics, so some plastic goods, such as cameras and film, are treated so fungi can't eat them. The following are some of fungi's most favorite things:

- wood
- cloth
- twine
- electrical insulation
- leather
- food products (*and* packaging)
- ink
- glue

- paint
- sponge
- cork
- dead animals and insects
- hair
- wool
- earwax

35

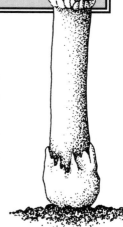

STINKHORNS

One of the most disgusting fungi grows in rotting wood. Called stinkhorns, they produce a smell like decaying flesh. Their thick stalk, which grows to a height of several inches, is topped with a liquid ball of jellylike, stinky slime. Flies, attracted by the smell, wallow in the slime, covering themselves with wet fungal spores. The insects fly away, depositing the spores where they land.

FUN FUNGI FACTS!

These Shoes Were Made for Eatin': Leather is one of a mold's favorite foods. Because leather goods retain a lot of moisture, shoes made from leather are continuously being eaten by microscopic molds inside them. You can't see this, because the digesting goes on inside the leather. But any shoe, after it has been worn for a while, has a heart of mold.

Fungi Flavor: Some fungi are used to flavor foods, such as Roquefort cheese, which was first created, possibly by accident, in the Roquefort area of France several hundred years ago. Traditionally, the cheese is stored in wooden casks in cool, moist limestone caves. Mold is added to the casks, where it thrives, digesting and rotting the cheese, giving it a tangy flavor. The ribbons of blue-green spots that mottle the cheese are the mold's reproductive cells.

Fungi Freeze: Fungi don't die from cold. In fact, many of them can live quite nicely at freezing temperatures. A home freezer has to keep food well below freezing (about 20 degrees Fahrenheit), or the food will get moldy. Meat stored in a butcher's freezer, which doesn't get as cold as a home freezer, will become covered with fungus if it stays there more than a few weeks.

GREENIES

We often think of plants as being nature's most beautiful adornment. But the reality is that some plants can be downright nauseating and foul-smelling. Read on to learn about nature's most disgusting plants, botanical barf inducers.

PUTRID PLANTS

Amorphophallus (a-mor-fo-FAL-us): The flower of this exotic plant from Sumatra can reach a height of

TASTELESS TRIVIA:

A fungus found in Washington state is the single largest living thing on Earth. Sprawling for 1,500 acres (2.5 square miles), it's the size of four hundred blue whales put together! The fungus lives about three feet underground, beneath the forested slopes of Mount Adams. This behemoth has been alive for centuries and, shudderingly, it moves inch by inch, growing ever bigger, devouring all dead organic matter (i.e., plants, woodland creatures, and possibly people) in its path.

eight feet. But its most notable feature is its nauseous stench, which has been compared to a combination of burnt sugar and rotten fish. The foul smell actually attracts flies, which pollinate the plant.

Aristolochia (a-ris-ti-LO-kee-a) grandiflora, or Pelican Flower: Found in Brazil and Jamaica, this huge plant is a decorator's nightmare: patchy purple-brown inside with a pale yellow-green outside. Its smell is so disgusting that wild animals stampede from the area when the plant blossoms.

Western False Hellebore: Found on the high mountain ranges of the northern Rockies, this plant is responsible for "monkey face" disease in newborn lambs. If a mother sheep eats this plant, her lambs will be born with deformed heads—the nose shortened or gone altogether, and the face caved in. In extreme cases, both eyeballs are in one eye socket in the middle of the lamb's forehead.

37

CRAWLIES

Worms, leeches, maggots, and virtually all creatures that crawl are pretty gross. Their names are gross, their looks are gross, but their behavior is the grossest thing of all.

LARVAE

When fly, roach, and other insect eggs hatch, the baby bugs don't come out looking like miniature versions of their parents. Instead these babies are tiny, white, squishy, sightless worms, called larvae.

Because larvae can't move far, the eggs must be laid on or near the source of the food the baby insects will need to grow.

FOUL FACT:

The aphid lion, the larva of the lacewing insect, eats tiny plant lice called aphids. After sucking the juice out of its prey, the aphid lion sticks the empty aphid corpses on the pointy hairs on its back. It then wears these gruesome decorations, adding more until they completely cover its body.

38

• Bluebottle flies lay their eggs on dead, decaying flesh, while gray flesh flies spread their squirming babies, called maggots, on the rotting meat that they will eat.

• Greenbottle flies lay their eggs in the open sores of living sheep. When the eggs hatch, the maggots crawl into the sheep's flesh and begin to eat it.

• Warble flies lay their eggs in the nasal passages of horses and other animals, where they live and eat the cartilage and flesh of the animals' noses.

• Houseflies leave their eggs on piles of dog manure, or rotting garbage if no manure is available. If a female housefly lays her eggs on a pile of manure and then decides to land on your lunch, she carries specks of manure ripe with millions of germs on the hairs of her legs and belly onto your food.

MAGGOT FEEDING TIME

Imagine this scene: You are walking through the woods when you suddenly hear an unidentifiable shushing sound. Curious, you push your way through the underbrush toward it, and what you find just about makes you lose your lunch. Thousands and thousands of maggots completely cover the rotting corpse of a woodland animal. The maggots form a layer so thick they appear to be a single rippling, living mass. An occasional ripple forces a ball of many maggots to roll off from the main mass.

How do maggots eat when their mouths have no hard parts—no teeth and no jaws? Maggots produce a liquid similar to human digestive juices that they spit onto the thing they desire to eat. The juices then digest the food to a liquid state, and the maggot slurps it up. One maggot produces enough of this juice to reduce a small cube of beef to a creamy brown puddle.

WASP LARVA 3, ROACH 0

Most insects go out and lay their eggs on or near food. Some wasps, on the other hand, bring food to their young. For example, one type of wasp will sting, thereby paralyzing but leaving alive, three cockroaches, which she'll then carry back to her nest. The wasp will lay an egg in the abdomen of one of the roaches, then fly away. Two days later, when the egg hatches, the wormlike larva will begin to eat the living flesh of the paralyzed roach. For two days it eats and eats and eats, concentrating on only the soft, juicy parts of its host and the other two roaches.

Finally, when all the soft pulp is gone, the larva will turn to the hard parts of the roaches, much as you may suck and chew on chicken bones after eating the meat. After five days, the larva is finished eating. It spins a tiny cocoon and emits, for the first time since it began eating, a lump of excrement. Over the next ten days, the larva becomes a fully formed wasp.

39

CATERPILLARS

Many insects protect themselves by mimicking other objects—some look like twigs on branches, others like the buds of flowers. One kind of caterpillar, or butterfly larva, protects itself by looking like bird feces. A glossy dark brown with a band of white down its back, it looks so much like fresh, moist bird poop that it sits out in the open and is rarely menaced by predators.

FOUL FACT:

Caterpillars seem to have many legs. But most of these are not real legs at all but muscular warts!

EARTHWORMS

Earthworms hibernate whenever the soil becomes too dry or too cold. They stop feeding, empty out their bowels, and make a little mucus-lined space for

themselves in the earth. Then they twist themselves into a ball, tuck their end into the center, and roll into their prepared space to sleep through the dry or cold spell.

If an earthworm breaks in two, it will regenerate the parts of its body that it lost, either the front or the back. Sometimes there is a malfunction in the worm, and the wrong part grows back—it might end up either with two tails or with a head at each end. These freaks don't live long.

LEECHES

Leeches are bloodsucking aquatic worms that were once commonly used in medicine for bloodletting. Bloodletting was a treatment first recorded by Greek physicians over two thousand years ago, practiced by doctors to cure diseases. A leech would be placed on the skin over the vein of the patient, where it would suck up about half an ounce of the person's blood.

While bloodletting fell out of favor in the late 1800s, doctors have recently found a new use for leeches following surgery. They are in many cases the safest, most effective way to remove extra blood from sensitive tissue, especially around the eyes, or after transplanting skin.

Fun Leech Facts!
- The type of leech used by doctors today is collected straight from freshwater ponds and streams.
- The medicinal leech is green with brown stripes, between two and four inches long when at rest, and twice as long while swimming.
- A leech's mouth has three jaws (as opposed to our two), each one with sixty to one hundred teeth. They attach themselves to their victims by biting into their flesh.
- A leech can drink up to eight times its weight in blood at one sitting!

NEMATODES

These tiny (about a millimeter long), transparent worms are little more than eating machines, digestive systems wrapped in skin. They live in almost all soil—in fact, there may be *thousands* of them in a spoonful of dirt. Some live inside the stomachs of other insects and eat the food their host is trying to digest. But turn-about is fair play—some fungi eat nematodes while the worm is still alive and wriggling. The fungus drills into the body of the living worm, starts growing inside it, and begins digesting the worm from the inside out.

CREEPIES

Insects. Their pulpy insides are held in place by their exoskeletons, or hard outer bodies. They walk on six legs and sometimes fly on two pairs of wings.

Insects don't have brains as such. Instead they have little knots of nerves, called ganglia, located near their various body parts. So an insect whose head has been bitten off can still fly or walk around for a while—it just won't have much reason for going anywhere! Read on to find out more about these creepiest of critters.

41

ANTS

Most ants eat only liquids. When they do take solids into their mouths, such as dust, dirt, pollen, or plant fragments, they keep them in a pouch in their jaw until they dissolve. They then swallow just the liquid part and spit out the remaining solids, usually onto the ant colony's compost heap, where fungus grows to feed the colony.

When a queen ant leaves a colony to start a new one, she brings with her a mouthful of the colony's fungus. When she finds a suitable new home, she digs a hole and spits out the fungus. She then lays a few eggs and crushes them into the fungus, mixing in some of her own dung. This gets the fungus growing. When she is satisfied that there is enough fungus for a colony, she

FOUL FACT:

In addition to the contents of their jaw pouches, ants add caterpillar dung, their own excrement, and dead ants to the compost heap.

TASTELESS TRIVIA:

The name "ear-wig" may come from the unwarranted fear that an earwig will enter the ear of a sleeping person and eat its way into the brain. On an episode of Rod Serling's "Night Gallery," aired in 1972, a man survives having an earwig eat through his brain. He finds out that the earwig was a female, and that it laid its eggs inside his head!

42

lays more eggs and allows them to hatch, thus beginning a new colony.

EARWIGS

Earwigs eat their prey alive. They will grasp a victim, a caterpillar for instance, with their rear pincers at one end and their pinching mouthparts at the other, and rip the caterpillar's body in half. The earwig will then eat the still struggling prey from the inside out.

FLEAS

The most notorious flea of all is the chigger, which lives in tropical climates. Instead of living on the skin, it digs under the skin of animals and humans, causing painful growths. The female lays eggs under the skin, and the young have to eat their way to the surface when they hatch.

FLIES

A housefly's mouthparts are soft, spongy things that can only sop up liquid food. So why does it bother landing on solid food, like hamburgers and french fries? In order for a fly to have liquid food to eat, it first throws up some of what it has previously eaten and partially digested—rotted garbage or dog manure, for instance—onto your burger and fries. This partly digested matter contains an acid that dissolves a bit of whatever the fly has landed on, making it possible for the fly to lap up a solid piece of food.

LOCUSTS

The seventeen-year locust spends sixteen years and nine months of its life underground and only three months of its life aboveground.

Occasionally, these locusts are attacked while underground by a parasite fungus. The parasite gets into the abdomen of the locust and eats its innards, turning them into clumps of powdery spores. The locust then emerges from the ground half-digested by the fungus. In response to this attack, the locust may, in vain, shed parts of its abdomen, to free itself of the voracious fungus, eventually leaving only the head and thorax (minus the third body segment of the locust) feebly fumbling around.

LICE

Head Lice: These tiny wingless parasites attach their eggs, white specks called nits, with a cliplike device to animal and human hairs. The nits are attached so solidly that even scratching or shaking the hair won't get them off. When the eggs hatch, the lice bite the scalp and drink the blood, causing itchy scabs to form.

Crab Lice: These lice live hidden in body hair, such as pubic, armpit, and even eyebrow hair. Their bites are intensely itchy. The brown specks seen stuck to the hair are their excrement.

Body Lice: These lice live in clothing and hop onto the body only to feed. They were such a common problem for American soldiers serving overseas during World War I that the GIs coined a name—"cooties"—for them.

43

The Dreaded Typhus
Body lice spread typhus. The symptoms are horrific, including a black tongue, skin eruptions, and vomit that is "black, like coffee badly boiled." In the 1930s, at the autopsy of a man who had died of typhus, the doctors began sawing the top of his skull off. So much pressure from the fever had built up inside the man's head that, before the doctors could finish the job, the top of his skull flew off!

MOSQUITOES

Mosquitoes can lay their eggs in any stagnant body of water, from a swamp to a muddy footprint. When the eggs hatch, the mosquito larvae wiggle around in the water like worms. After about a week, the adult mosquitoes rise from the water in search of fresh blood.

How Mosquitoes Carry Diseases

The rubbery flesh of the mosquito's nose covers six tiny needles inside. The mosquito pulls back this fleshy sheath when it bites, opening a wound in its victim. Immediately upon biting, the mosquito injects saliva, which contains a mild anesthetic, into its prey. Mosquito saliva also contains a substance that keeps blood from clotting, so the mosquito can drink freely. Left to drink, the mosquito will take in its weight in blood at one sitting. Mosquitoes occasionally inject other things into their victims' bloodstreams—like the parasite that causes malaria.

SPITTLEBUGS

Those puffs of bubbly foam that you see clinging to the stems of tall grass are the whipped spit of spittlebugs. Female spittlebugs lay their eggs on grass stems. When the eggs hatch, the babies crawl up the grass and emit a tiny drop of saliva. They dip their rear ends into the drop of spit and begin blowing bubbles in it with air expelled from their anuses, whipping the drop of spittle up into a frothy mass. Then the spittlebug babies hide inside the bubbles, eating small insects that get caught in the sticky foam.

WATER BUGS

TASTELESS TRIVIA: In Brazil, giant water bugs can be up to *half a foot* long!

Giant water bugs live in fresh water and look like huge cockroaches. Two to three inches long on the average, they are fierce creatures who kill fish, frogs, and anything they can get their little claws on. They grasp tightly, plunge their needle-like jaws into their victim, and suck out its blood.

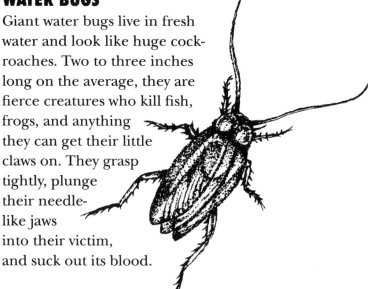

44

HOUSE OF HORRORS

So you think your bedroom is a safe haven from the grossness around you? Don't bet on it. No room in your house is free of grossness. Read on to learn about the creatures you spend your waking—and sleeping—moments with!

BEDROOM

You share your bed with at least one million dust mites. They are invisible to the naked eye, but they're there—living under your sheets, eating, breeding, and dying. (I.e., you share your bed with thousands of *corpses* of dust mites.) Millions more live in your carpets.

Mites dine on the skin flakes that fall from you and your family. Each one produces about twenty pellets of feces a day. With every step you take, thousands of these pellets are propelled into the air. People who have frequent sneezing fits are often allergic to dust mite feces without knowing it.

45

Vacuuming Can Be Gross
Vacuuming is one of the best ways to spray billions of mite fecal pellets through the air of your house. The fecal pellets are so tiny they easily slip through invisible cracks in the paper fibers of the vacuum bag. After they are sucked up by the vacuum cleaner, the pellets spew right out of the cleaner's exhaust and into the air, where they can float for days.

In addition, the dust mites themselves are sucked into the vacuum cleaner, where they can live contentedly inside the vacuum bag for hundreds of generations.

KITCHEN

Everywhere you look in the kitchen, you can find disgusting, nauseating life forms—if you are equipped with microscopic vision, of course.

Sponge: An ordinary kitchen sponge is crawling with millions of bacteria, feeding on grease and on the sponge itself. Even worse, they are easily spread to any surface wiped by the sponge— countertops, tables, refrigerators, and everywhere else, where they begin to multiply.

Refrigerator: If you have ever tasted sour milk, that means you were sipping the waste of millions of bacteria swimming in the old milk.

Stovetop: All sorts of grisly matter is constantly falling into open pots on the stovetop, including dust (made up of skin flakes, flies' eyes, spider legs, and more), dust mite corpses, and mite fecal pellets.

BATHROOM

No doubt the grossest room in the house, the bathroom is constantly being assaulted by dangerous bacteria each time the toilet is flushed. With each flush, a fine mist consisting of billions of water droplets rises into the air. Hundreds of thousands of these droplets contain bacteria from our intestines. These bacteria land on every surface of the bathroom—floors, cabinets, sink, doorknob, even your toothbrush.

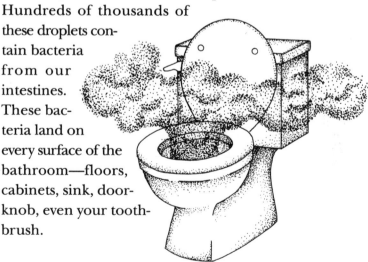

THE GAGGING GOURMET

Food. We need to eat it to survive. And to many people, eating certain foods is one of life's greatest pleasures. But not all foods are appetizing to everyone, and some foods are downright disgusting to many. Bugs, ape brains, jellyfish—you might think people would never eat those things on purpose, but they do. And even worse are the things we all eat every day without realizing it!

THE MOST NAUSEATING FOODS IN THE WORLD

All around the world, people are eating and enjoying foods that would make you and your friends puke!

IN ALASKA

At least until the middle of this century, the Inuit Indians considered the partly digested green vegetables and grasses taken from the stomachs of animals they killed to be a great delicacy.

The Inuits also put the fins, heads, tails, and guts of fish in earthenware pots that they buried underground, letting the contents decay for several months. When

FOUL FACT:

In ancient times, there were several problems associated with buying and keeping brains: they spoiled quickly, were hard to digest, and apparently even the people who ate them found their taste disgusting. Medieval brain-eaters solved these problems by adding plenty of salt and lots of spices like oregano.

dug up and ready to serve, this dish has the consistency of thick paste and a flavor like pungent cheese.

IN ANCIENT EUROPE

In medieval times, people ate animal brains, believing that they helped to build thick, healthy blood, and also that they kept the eater's brain healthy.

IN ANCIENT ROME

The ancient Romans loved to eat, and on special occasions they were known for their extravagant meals. The menu for one particularly lavish feast included pike liver, pheasant brain, peacock brain, flamingo tongue, and lamprey eggs.

IN CHINA

Among the delicacies sold today in the markets of China are:

- Swallows' nests, for use in bird's nest soup. The nests are made by a variety of swallow that lives near the sea. It mixes its saliva with meat pecked from decaying fish, and then drools thin, sticky threads, which are woven into a nest. The nests are sold dry, and they expand when they are soaked, giving the soup a thick quality.

- Dried jellyfish, sold in thin, almost transparent strips.
- "Vegetable caterpillar," a fungus that has eaten the flesh of a certain kind of caterpillar and is sold encased in the caterpillar's skin.
- Bear paws, eaten on special occasions at Chinese banquets.

IN ENGLAND

Jellied eels, cut into three- or four-inch-long pieces, are purchased from street vendors. They are a favorite snack of young and old alike.

IN FRANCE

Truffles, fungi spread by rodents, insects, and pigs, are considered a great delicacy by gourmets around the world. They grow underground, a smelly mass of spores in a thick skin. Because they grow about a half a foot under the ground, they have to be hunted by scent. Professional truffle hunters use pigs to hunt the tasty fungi. The pigs alert them to the truffles' scent by snorting up a storm and digging at the ground. Hunters then gently dig up the valuable spores themselves. The biggest, smelliest, most "delicious" truffles come from southern France and northern Italy.

TASTELESS TRIVIA:

Roman gourmets would fatten the larvae of stag beetles on flour and wine and then eat them.

49

The Truth About Truffles

Fungal spores, which make up most of a truffle, remain undigested as they travel through a person's or animal's digestive tract. The spores are expelled, intact, in the feces. This is how truffles are spread around by animals in the wild, as more truffles grow wherever the animal's droppings land. (Truffles need thick soil rich in nutrients to grow, which is why they don't grow in our sewers. If a person who ate a truffle were to defecate in the woods, a truffle would likely grow.)

IN GERMANY

Blood from cows, goats, and sheep is eaten in the dish "fried blood," and is also used in making blood pudding, a type of sausage.

IN IRELAND

Since the 1600s, Ireland's version of blood pudding is made by bleeding cows and boiling the blood with milk, butter, and herbs. In some places, the fresh blood was allowed to clot, then preserved with salt, cut into squares, and put aside as food for the winter.

IN SCOTLAND

Haggis, a traditional Scottish food, is a pudding made from the ground heart, lungs, and liver of a sheep mixed with oatmeal and fat. The mixture is stuffed into the sheep's stomach, and is tied off. The stomach is then placed in a pot of water and boiled. Haggis is eaten in Scotland on national holidays.

IN TAIWAN

Fresh raw ape brains are considered a delicacy to the Taiwanese. The dead ape's skull is broken with a stone or wooden hammer, and the brain is scooped out with a china or bamboo spoon. The brains are considered to be a "brain food," which will improve the intelligence of a person who eats them.

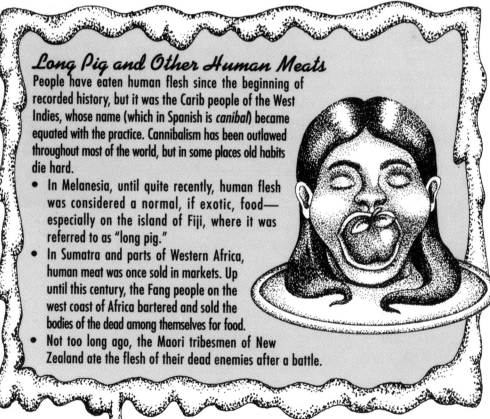

Long Pig and Other Human Meats

People have eaten human flesh since the beginning of recorded history, but it was the Carib people of the West Indies, whose name (which in Spanish is *caníbal*) became equated with the practice. Cannibalism has been outlawed throughout most of the world, but in some places old habits die hard.

- In Melanesia, until quite recently, human flesh was considered a normal, if exotic, food—especially on the island of Fiji, where it was referred to as "long pig."
- In Sumatra and parts of Western Africa, human meat was once sold in markets. Up until this century, the Fang people on the west coast of Africa bartered and sold the bodies of the dead among themselves for food.
- Not too long ago, the Maori tribesmen of New Zealand ate the flesh of their dead enemies after a battle.

FOOD FOR THOUGHT

What disgusting foods do *you* eat? None? Think again. Take a look at some of the gross stuff you routinely put in your mouth.

CEREAL KILLER

Check out the side panel on your favorite box of breakfast cereal. See the ingredients? They don't look especially gross, do they? Well, wait till you learn where some of them come from!

- *Gelatin:* A thickener that comes from the skins, hooves, and skeletons of pigs and cows.
- *Whey:* The thin, watery, yellow liquid that remains after the protein is removed from milk.
- *Glycerin:* A substance left over after manufacturing soap.
- *Artificial flavors:* More than a thousand different kinds of man-made chemicals are used to flavor food.
- *Natural colors:* Natural colors come from plants and animals, including tropical birds, fish, and insects. Carmine, a red dye, comes from the dried, crushed bodies of female scale insects.
- *Artificial colors:* Artificial colors are dyes made from coal tar and petroleum.

51

MUSHROOMS

So you like mushrooms on your pizza? These tasty fungi have been grown for food in the Western Hemisphere for the last four hundred years. Disgusting as it may seem, the mushrooms you eat are grown on piles of fresh horse manure. The manure is heated for days until it turns into crumbly compost. It is then spread into beds and sprinkled with mushroom spores—the reproductive part of the mushroom. The spores are then covered with soil. After a few weeks, tiny mushrooms appear, which soon grow to maturity.

HOLD THE BUTTER

Nowadays, we can be fairly certain the butter we eat is reasonably fresh and pure. That wasn't always the case. Until recent decades, sanitary conditions at dairies were sickening.

Mold was a big problem—inspectors often found cream covered by up to half an inch of mold. The cream (*and* mold) would then be churned into butter, which before long would be covered by festive yellow, green, pink, and brown fur.

But mold wasn't the only thing found in the cream. Cans of cream with drowned rats in them were not uncommon—one creamery owner told the inspectors that he found a rat in one can of cream that was so bloated he had to puncture its dead body to get it out!

The facilities at the creameries could be just as disgusting as their end products. Water used to wash the butter was often contaminated by sewage, the vats the cream was poured in were full of mold, and the entire premises were a breeding place for flies. Inspectors found so many maggots in one pound of butter that if they were laid end to end, the maggots would have stretched eleven feet.

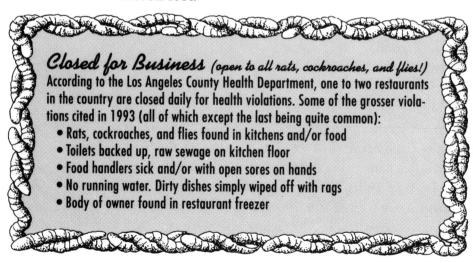

Closed for Business (open to all rats, cockroaches, and flies!)
According to the Los Angeles County Health Department, one to two restaurants in the country are closed daily for health violations. Some of the grosser violations cited in 1993 (all of which except the last being quite common):
- Rats, cockroaches, and flies found in kitchens and/or food
- Toilets backed up, raw sewage on kitchen floor
- Food handlers sick and/or with open sores on hands
- No running water. Dirty dishes simply wiped off with rags
- Body of owner found in restaurant freezer

PASS THE PIG'S FEET

After a pig is slaughtered and the commercially salable cuts of meat like hams and bacon are taken away and packaged, there is a carcassful of usable pig parts left. As someone once said, the only part of the pig they haven't found a use for is the squeal. Take a look at this list of edible meat by-products from hogs:

- Brains, cheeks, head meat, and tongues are used for headcheese.
- The pancreas is sold as sweetbreads.
- Intestines are used as casings for sausages and hot dogs.
- Ears, faces, hearts, kidneys, lips, eyelids, esophaguses, livers, snouts, stomachs, and tails end up in sausages and hot dogs.
- Feet are chilled and sold fresh, or pickled as a delicacy.
- Skeletons are rendered into gelatin.

53

Truth in Advertising

The pancreas of a calf is considered by some to be a delicacy and is even served at some fancy restaurants. But don't expect to see "pancreas" on the menu. Apparently, the original chefs who cooked this organ wanted to entice their patrons, so they came up with a much more pleasant sounding name—sweetbreads. Sweetbreads may also consist of the thymus, salivary, and lymphatic glands, but the pancreas is most common. Animals other than the calf may contribute their glands, but sweetbread eaters seem to like the calf's best.

CREEPING CUISINE

Some bugs bite people—but did you know that many people bite bugs? Only in North America and Europe do people find the idea of eating bugs revolting. In other countries of the world, insects provide a large part of the diet. And not just because insects are the only available food—many people find them quite delicious!

BEST BUGS

From ancient times to the present, people have eaten bugs. But the bugs eaten differ from place to place. The following is a list of who eats what and where. (Except as indicated, people in these countries—especially in the small rural villages—still eat them.)

Africa (central) Paste made from caterpillars or palmworms and wrapped in a large leaf; beetles, termites, locusts, and gnats molded into cakes and dried.

Australia The abdomens of honey ants, swollen with honey, are bitten off. Grubs, some as long as three inches and thick as a man's finger, are eaten alive or lightly roasted.

China Silkworm pupae, a by-product of silk production, are dried over a fire, then cooked in butter or oil. Sometimes eggs are added and they are made into an omelet. Water beetles are eaten fried. Caterpillars and fly and ant maggots are considered delicacies. Giant water bugs are boiled in hot brine and eaten after removing the legs and other hard parts.

Grasshoppers are de-winged, the head is removed along with the intestines, and the insect is fried with salt.

India A paste is made of the green tree ant and eaten as a condiment with curry. Red ants are pounded into a pulpy mass, mixed with salt and chili, and eaten raw with boiled rice.

Japan Grasshoppers are boiled in salty water, and earthworms are made into pies.

Java Beetle grubs—"thick white maggots"—are stuck on a stick and roasted; dragonflies (head, wings, and legs removed) are fried with onions and shrimp. Women pick lice from their friends' heads and eat the lice—alive.

Malaya Grubs found in cattle dung are collected and fried. The maggots and eggs of honeybees are boiled with a honeycomb, making a prized soup.

55

Mexico The ancient Aztecs ate bee maggots with wild honey and grasshoppers cooked into stews. Today, ant maggots and caterpillars are eaten either raw or cooked. Insect eggs are ground into flour and baked into a bread called *huatlé.*

South America Along the Amazon River, people eat the great-headed ant—alive. Holding the creature by the head, they bite off the fatty abdomen. Head lice, a great delicacy, are also eaten alive.

United States As late as the 1920s, Native Americans of the Great Basin Region prepared caterpillars in soup, or fried them crisp and brown. Maggots were dried, then crushed into a powder and baked into cakes.

West Indies Weevil grubs (called "gru-gru") are roasted; palmworms are breaded with flour, fried, and served with orange juice. Butter is made out of palmworm fat.

BUG OFF

In May 1992, the New York Entomological Society, whose professional and amateur members study insects, met for a banquet to celebrate the society's one hundredth anniversary. As so many cultures around the world make bugs and other insects a regular part of their diet, the society decided it was only fitting that they plan a menu featuring a variety of international insect dishes.

Waiters moved around the banquet room offering trays of fried mealworms and crickets to guests. According to some, the mealworms tasted "fruity" and the crickets were "crunchy, like potato chips."

Also on the menu were:
- giant Thai water bugs—three-inch-long cousins of the common American cockroach—sautéed in olive oil
- cricket-and-vegetable tempura
- wild mushrooms in mealworm flour
- worm balls in spicy tomato sauce
- roasted Australian grubs (which were described as "juicy little sausages with a mouth at one end")

For dessert, a rich chocolate cricket torte and insect sugar cookies were served. Live honey ants were also a very popular dessert. The ants had been fed on peach juice, and their abdomens were swollen with golden nectar, which is why they are popularly known as honeypot ants. Guests stood in line for the chance to catch them with a pair of tweezers. "They taste like candy," said one diner.

Gene DeFoliart, Ph.D., professor of entomology at the University of Wisconsin, organized, and spoke at, the banquet. Dr. DeFoliart publishes the *Food Insects Newsletter* three times a year. He believes that insects are a nutritious but often overlooked source of food that may help to ease the food shortage problems caused by overpopulation. The newsletter includes insect recipes and helpful tips such as where to find bugs, as well as the best time to collect them. If you want a copy of the most recent newsletter, write to Gene DeFoliart, Ph.D., at the following address:

> University of Wisconsin
> 237 Russell Lab
> 1630 Linden Drive
> Madison, Wisconsin 53706

Bon appétit!

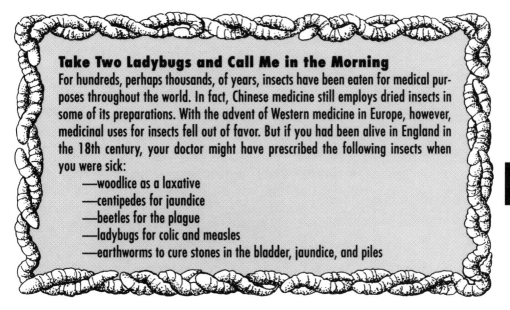

Take Two Ladybugs and Call Me in the Morning

For hundreds, perhaps thousands, of years, insects have been eaten for medical purposes throughout the world. In fact, Chinese medicine still employs dried insects in some of its preparations. With the advent of Western medicine in Europe, however, medicinal uses for insects fell out of favor. But if you had been alive in England in the 18th century, your doctor might have prescribed the following insects when you were sick:

—woodlice as a laxative
—centipedes for jaundice
—beetles for the plague
—ladybugs for colic and measles
—earthworms to cure stones in the bladder, jaundice, and piles

WAITER, THERE'S A FLY IN MY SOUP—AND IT TASTES GREAT

In most restaurants, it is a terrible thing to find a bug in your food. But there is one restaurant in Washington, D.C., where you'd be disappointed if you didn't find one. The restaurant is called The Insect Club, and it has been serving insect cuisine since 1992.

Mealworm wontons and chimichangas, cricket meatloaf and burgers—these are just some of the buggy items on the menu. In the mood for an appetizer? How about spicy candied mealworm and cricket popcorn? And how about a piece of cricket brittle for dessert? That's right, cricket brittle. It's like peanut brittle, only with crickets instead of peanuts.

"All the bug dishes are very popular," says chef Mark Nevin. "I go through 20,000 mealworms and 8,000 crickets every two weeks."

Nevin's idea is to show that insects can be eaten as normal food. He doesn't go in for fried grubs or any dish where an insect is recognizable as an insect. By roasting and grinding the creepy-crawly critters into flour, using the flour in muffins and cakes, and baking bugs into other dishes, Nevin hopes he can get the public used to eating insects.

Of course, it took some trial and error to get the recipes right. And he and the restaurant staff had to taste the food as he was first creating it to make sure the dishes were not only edible but delicious. Apparently he has been successful, because many customers are regulars who return again and again.

Nevin does have one problem that most chefs don't have, however—when he puts an ingredient down on the counter, he never knows if it will stay put!

OVER THE LIPS AND PAST THE GUMS

So, how does a taco or hot fudge sundae with the works turn into urine and feces? Read this description of the digestive process and find out!

INTO THE MOUTH . . .

First food is chewed, torn, and ground up by the teeth. The salivary glands, which empty into the mouth through little tubes, add digestive enzymes into the food as it is chewed. Once the food is a squishy-soft mass, it will easily slide down your throat with a little push from the tongue.

... DOWN THE THROAT ...

The throat is the passage that leads from the mouth to the stomach, nose, and the lungs. The last thing you want is ground beef and shredded lettuce coming out of your nose, so a complex system of fleshy trapdoors and levers in the throat swings into action when you swallow. The trapdoors force the food to travel a path toward the esophagus, the tube surrounded by muscles that squeezes food down the throat. At the bottom end of the esophagus is a valve that opens to allow food to plop, bit by bit, into the stomach.

... INTO THE STOMACH ...

The stomach is a stretchy pouch, a holding tank for food until the small intestine is ready for it. Food sits in the stomach for four to six hours, breaking down as it is covered with digestive juices. (Rennin, one of the digestive juices, curdles milk in our stomachs. Another digestive juice is hydrochloric acid, a chemical strong enough to burn a hole through a piece of wood.) Some glands produce mucus, which surrounds the particles of food, making them slimy enough to ease their way into the small intestine. The walls of the stomach contract in waves every twenty seconds or so, gently pushing the partially dissolved food toward the small intestine.

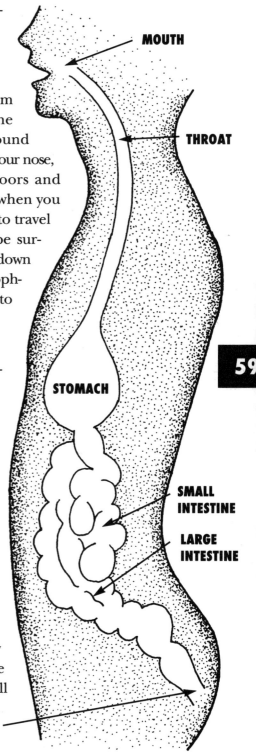

MOUTH

THROAT

59

STOMACH

SMALL INTESTINE

LARGE INTESTINE

RECTUM

FOUL FACT:

Children under the age of ten produce more feces for their weight every day than adults do.

TASTELESS TRIVIA:

It is not absolutely necessary to have a stomach to live—some people have had their stomachs completely removed. They have to eat lightly, however, because the food goes straight from their esophagus to their small intestine.

60

. . . THROUGH THE SMALL INTESTINE . . .

The small intestine is a twenty-five- to thirty-five-foot (approximate adult size) tube where most of the digestion, the body's process of breaking down food into nutrients, takes place. The watery gruel from the stomach—it's called "chyme" (kime)—moves down the small intestine at the rate of about an inch a minute. The muscles of the small intestine squeeze and release, forcing the chyme along, much like the way you squeeze toothpaste from a tube. As the small intestine breaks down the chyme, the intestine's inner lining absorbs its usable nutrients. After five hours or so, ninety-five percent of all the digestible matter in the chyme has been digested. The remaining unusable chyme, mostly consisting of water, cellulose, and fiber, then enters the large intestine.

. . . AROUND THE LARGE INTESTINE . . .

About twelve ounces of watery chyme leave the small intestine every day and enter the large intestine, or colon. This material then takes about another day to pass through the two- to three-foot length of the large intestine. During this part of the chyme's journey, water is gradually absorbed into the intestinal wall and returned to the body, leaving an ever-drier mass to be pushed along the length of the intestine. Of the twelve ounces of waste that enter the large intestine daily, only four ounces of feces remain at the end to enter the rectum.

. . . AND INTO THE RECTUM.

Slowly the rectum fills with feces, causing a feeling of pressure and the need to go to the bathroom. As waste material begins to collect in the rectum, the muscles of the colon begin contracting faster, rapidly filling the rectum with more waste. Once full, you open your sphincter (the muscle that usually keeps the anus shut tight), defecation takes place, and the rectum is emptied.

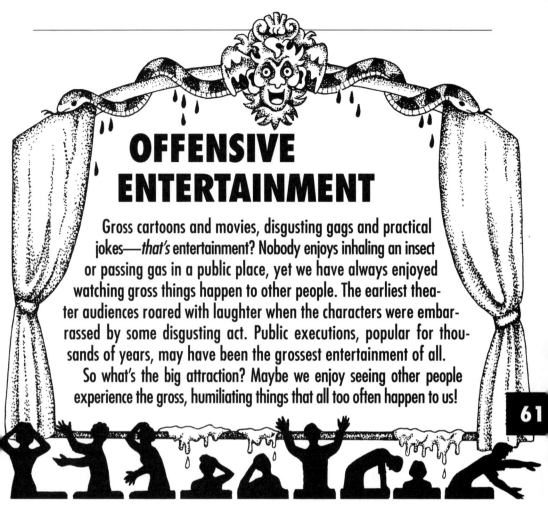

OFFENSIVE ENTERTAINMENT

Gross cartoons and movies, disgusting gags and practical jokes—*that's* entertainment? Nobody enjoys inhaling an insect or passing gas in a public place, yet we have always enjoyed watching gross things happen to other people. The earliest theater audiences roared with laughter when the characters were embarrassed by some disgusting act. Public executions, popular for thousands of years, may have been the grossest entertainment of all.

So what's the big attraction? Maybe we enjoy seeing other people experience the gross, humiliating things that all too often happen to us!

THE GROSSEST SCENES ON SCREEN

Which would you rather see—a moving love story or a movie so disgusting you have to turn away from the screen? Since you're reading this book, it is pretty obvious which you'd prefer. So without further ado, here are ten of the grossest scenes in the history of cinema that you don't want to miss.

THE FLY (ORIGINAL, 1958, AND REMAKE, 1986)

The silly original has a scene that retains a gross fascination in spite of its absurdity—a tiny fly, with the head of a man, is caught in a spider web and is about to be sucked dry by a spider. "Help me, help me," the high-pitched little fly-man squeals.

The remake features one of the most disgusting scenes in recent memory. The scientist-turned-fly, played by Jeff Goldblum, proves his dilemma to a doubting doctor by throwing up acid on the doctor's arm, dissolving it into a liquid mass, and then eating the arm!

A MAN CALLED HORSE (1970)

Richard Harris plays Lord John Morgan, an aristocrat captured by Sioux Indians. In time, Lord Morgan wants to join the tribe, but to do so he must pass the tribe's initiation rite. This rite is the film's most grueling scene, for both Harris *and* the moviegoer. The skin on Harris's chest is pierced with iron needles, and he is hung overnight from ropes strung through his chest muscles.

THE GODFATHER (1972)

There is one scene that puts *The Godfather,* arguably the most powerful gangster film ever made, on this list: A film mogul who runs afoul of the mob wakes up in the middle of the night and feels a wet lump at the foot of his bed. Throwing back the covers, he finds the severed head of his beloved racehorse swimming in a pool of blood.

THE EXORCIST (1973)

This film became notorious in the 1970s for causing moviegoers to run out of theaters and throw up. An exorcist (a person, usually a priest, who expels demons that are possessing human beings) tries to rid a little girl, played by Linda Blair, of the demon inside her. The youngster projectile-vomits green puke all over the priest's face and clothes. Later, during the exorcism, the girl's skin splits and cracks and her head turns completely around on her neck.

NATIONAL LAMPOON'S ANIMAL HOUSE (1978)

This film features wacky chaos in a college fraternity house. The grossest scene takes place during lunch: John Belushi squeezes his cheeks together and spits out a huge wad of mashed potatoes. His explanation: he was doing an impression of a pimple.

ALL THAT JAZZ (1979)

Joe Gideon, the main character of this film, played by Roy Scheider, undergoes open-heart surgery, which we see on-camera. A doctor slices open what we think is Joe Gideon's chest and pulls back the skin, revealing the bone and muscle underneath. The doctor takes a tool with metal jaws and shoves it into a gap in the patient's breastbone. The doctor then turns a crank, splitting open the breastbone and revealing the beating heart underneath. This was no special effect—a real operation on an actual heart patient (*not* Roy Scheider!) was filmed for use in the movie.

63

THE TIN DRUM (1979)

A moving and odd film from Germany, *The Tin Drum* contains one especially gross scene. The main character, a young boy, and his family are watching a man fishing with a thick rope. They ask him what he is fishing for. "Watch," he says mysteriously. He pulls and pulls on the rope, finally pulling a rotted horse's head from the water. Just as we, the movie audience, are gasping from surprise, several thick, slimy eels dart out of the horse's empty eye sockets and mouth. At least one of the characters in the film throws up (as do many moviegoers!).

POLTERGEIST (1982)

A team of psychic researchers come to study a house that is being plagued by a poltergeist, which, according to folklore, is a mischievous ghost. Some current researchers in the paranormal, or supernatural, however, believe a poltergeist to be unfocused psychic energy.

In the movie, one of the researchers sleeps at the house, and in the middle of the night goes to fix himself a snack. The steak he pulls from the freezer begins crawling on the counter, and suddenly hundreds of maggots spew from it. The young researcher goes into the bathroom to wash up, and in the mirror, he sees that his face seems to be peeling. He starts to pick at it, and all the flesh from his face suddenly peels away, revealing the skull beneath his skin.

MONTY PYTHON'S THE MEANING OF LIFE (1983)

This movie contains the longest sustained on-camera vomiting sequence on record. The most obese man in the world enters his favorite restaurant and requests a bucket from the helpful waiter. As the man gorges on dish after dish, he continuously vomits into the bucket to make room for more food.

THE BLOB (REMAKE, 1988)

Although there's a soft spot in the hearts of horror movie fans for the original *Blob* (made in 1958), it doesn't hold a candle to the remake in terms of sheer grossness. While in the original movie the monster discreetly dragged its victims off-screen to digest them, the remake brings this consumption on-screen in all its gory glory. The Blob, a huge gelatinous mass, surrounds a human being and covers him with digestive juices, digesting him in full view of the film audience.

GROSS CARTOONS

Who is the grossest cartoon team in existence today? Although there are plenty of gross "underground" comic characters in the cartoons of R. Crumb, Ralph Bakshi, and others, gross is also entering prime time. Three of the most mainstream contenders in the gross sweepstakes are . . .

REN AND STIMPY (CREATED IN 1989 BY JOHN KRICFALUSI, DEBUTED IN 1991)

This cartoon dog and cat pair, appearing in their own series on the Nickelodeon cable network, defined a new standard for gross.

- No bodily function is below them—they pass wind in the bathtub, when they bend over, and whenever they get excited.
- Stimpy spits up hairballs and eats his kitty litter. He proudly displays his soiled cat box to Ren and the audience. He also spits toothpaste into jars and saves it.

ITCHY AND SCRATCHY (CREATED IN 1990 BY MATT GROENING)

A cartoon within a cartoon, "The Itchy and Scratchy Show" is Bart and Lisa Simpson's favorite TV show. Itchy is a mouse and Scratchy is a cat. In their never-ending battle with each other, Itchy always wins in some gross way:

- Itchy pulls Scratchy's still-beating heart out of his chest and gives it to Scratchy as a valentine.
- Itchy dresses as a minister and marries Scratchy and his cat bride, then cuts off their heads and drives away, with the severed cat heads dangling from his car instead of tin cans.
- Itchy pushes Scratchy into the firebox of an old-time steamboat, waits a moment, then gleefully pulls Scratchy's charred skull out of the flames.

- Itchy runs over Scratchy and Scratchy Jr. with a combine harvester, then plays catch with Itchy Jr., using Scratchy's head as the ball.

BEAVIS AND BUTT-HEAD (CREATED IN 1992 BY MIKE JUDGE)

Disgusting and dumb, and proud of it, Beavis and Butt-head (appearing on MTV) are America's favorite couch potatoes. On the few occasions they actually *do* venture into the world, something always seems to go grossly wrong:

- In an ill-fated attempt to kill an insect with a chainsaw, Beavis inadvertently slices off Butt-head's finger. Rather than seek emergency medical treatment, the two play a rousing set of air guitar tunes, as Butt-head's finger gushes blood everywhere.
- Butt-head knocks Beavis's face onto a hot griddle. When Beavis stands up, his flesh sticks to the hot metal and tears off.

GROSS ENTERTAINERS

All of us do disgusting things on occasion—usually by accident. Some schoolyard clowns do sick stuff on purpose to make other people laugh. But there are a few adults who actually get *paid* to be gross. It's their life's work. Read on to find some of the world's most famous professional gross-meisters.

THE ORIGINAL GROSSEST SHOW ON EARTH

In 1841, P. T. Barnum opened the American Museum, an exhibition of "freaks," curiosities, impossible animals (i.e., two-headed monstrosities), and the like. The "freaks" on display included Siamese twins, bearded ladies, and General Tom Thumb, the most famous little person of the 19th century.

Barnum freely made up wild histories and background stories for the people he exhibited, and used these fantastic fictions to generate publicity for the museum. He advertised everywhere and in every way he could think of. By 1850, his museum was a huge success, and by the time it was destroyed by fire in 1868, more than 41 million people had passed through its doors in hopes of being grossed out. (P. T. Barnum is best remembered for the circus named after him, which he immodestly called "The Greatest Show on Earth." The circus later merged with other circuses, and is today known as the Ringling Brothers and Barnum and Bailey Circus.)

LE PETOMANE ("THE FARTISTE")

Joseph Pujol, or Le Petomane, as he was known professionally, was a French vaudevillian who did impressions, played music, and smoked cigarettes, via air expelled from his anus. Born in 1857, Pujol discovered as a youth that he could suck up as much as two quarts of water, or air, into his rectum. He could hold the air or water inside him and expel it at his leisure. After a brief career as a baker, Pujol was hired in 1892 to be a performer at the famous Parisian music hall, the Moulin Rouge.

On stage, Le Petomane would imitate the farts of people in different circumstances, and after inserting (offstage) a tube into his anus, he would "smoke" a cigarette with his emissions, and play popular tunes of the day on an instrument like a kazoo. The air Pujol expelled was odorless, thanks to a daily enema. Enormously popular, Pujol performed for royalty, traveled the world, and eventually opened his own theater. He died in 1945 at the age of eighty-eight.

PENN AND TELLER

This team of magicians have become famous for their off-center, unpredictable magic act on stage, along with their TV appearances, films, and videos. They also have a well-earned reputation as practical jokers, and are known far and wide for the gross jokes they play on people. For instance, they once dumped thousands of live cockroaches on talk show host David Letterman's desk during a television broadcast.

In their books and videotapes, Penn and Teller give step-by-step instructions for some of their grossest gags. For example, in their book *How to Play with Your Food,* they describe how to make a heart-shaped jello mold that bleeds when it is sliced, and how to pretend to eat live ants.

JIM ROSE CIRCUS SIDESHOW

This troupe opens for rock shows, such as the 1992 Lollapalooza Tour, performing feats so disgusting they border on the dangerous. They also have a video-tape available called "The Jim Rose Traveling Sideshow."

If you have the opportunity (or the stomach) to see the Jim Rose Circus Sideshow in person, you may see:

- Matt ("The Tube") Crowley suck up huge quantities of chocolate sauce and ketchup through a straw in his nose, then spew them at the crowd.
- Jim Rose, a.k.a. Jimmy the Geek, place a massive railroad spike in his nostril and drive it up his nose with a sledgehammer.
- The Amazing Mr. Lifto suspend a cinder block from chains attached to rings piercing his chest. For good measure, he will slide a coat hanger through a hole in his tongue.
- The Torture King transform himself into a human pincushion. Then he will walk up a ladder with sharp blades for rungs.

BOYS AND GIRLS, TAKE CARE! DON'T TRY THESE STUNTS AT HOME!

GROSS NATIONAL PRODUCTS

Did you know that you can buy fake edible snot, soap that will make your face and hands turn bloody, and even artificial whale vomit? The following are some of the grossest toys and novelties you can (and could, in the recent past) buy:

GROSS TOYS

- *Creepy Crawlers* (manufactured by Mattel in the mid-1960s to late 1970s): By pouring liquid plastic into molds and heating it in a "Thingmaker," you could manufacture insects of every gross kind. Other Creepy Crawler sets created shrunken heads, skeletons, and other delightful items.

- *Slime* (manufactured by Mattel and sold in the 1980s): Sold in a miniature garbage can, this green slimy substance flowed disgustingly through your fingers and could be held out menacingly at younger brothers and sisters. Slime was also used in one widespread practical joke: First you placed a small amount of Slime in the palm of your hand, then, in front of a friend you made hideous throat-clearing sounds. After making a phlegm-rattling cough into your fist, you then opened your fist, held out your palm to your friend, and said, "Look!"

- *Monster Face* (manufactured by Mattel in 1991): A toy skull to which you can add creepy and disgusting eyes, noses, and mouths. By pressing on a pump at the back of the skull, you can make slime pour out of holes in the skull, to drip over the face you have just created.

- *Mortal Kombat* (Midway Manufacturing, 1992): The object of this gory video game is to kill your opponent with any one of a variety of "death

69

moves." When you pull your opponent's head off, his still-twitching spinal cord hangs from his severed neck. You can also rip the still-beating heart out of your opponent's chest, or reduce him to a charred skeleton with a lightning bolt.

CANDY

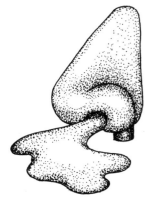

- *Gummy Worms and Gummy Rats:* the gross answer to the insipid Gummy Bears.

- *Snot* (manufactured by How Can It Be So Sour Company, 1993): a green jellylike candy that comes in a plastic nose. You eat it by pulling it, bit by bit, from the nostrils.

ADAMS NOVELTIES

The granddaddy of all gross novelties (gag gifts and jokes) is the S. S. Adams Company. The company began in 1906 when Sam Adams found a coal tar derivative that made people sneeze. He sold bags of it for a dime as "sneezing powder." The gag caught on—a tiny amount in the air could reduce an entire theater to helpless sneezing.

"Itching powder" came next, derived from a weed that grows in India. The favorite place to sprinkle this substance was on toilet seats.

Here are just a few of the most famous gross gags that Adams has developed through the years:

- the fly in the ice cube
- fake vomit
- fake dog poop
- the whoopee cushion (a person unknowingly sits on it and produces a loud, wet-sounding burst of air, which sounds remarkably like passing gas)
- jumping bloody bandage (a spring-loaded bandage is placed over a finger and released at an unsuspecting victim)

- black soap (when a person washes with this seemingly normal bar of white soap, his or her hands and face get *dirtier*)
- bloody soap (same as above, except this soap turns you into a bloody mess)
- the snake in the can (can looks as if it is filled with candy, but a spring-loaded snake pops out instead)

You can find these S. S. Adams gags and the many other magic tricks they manufacture at magic and novelty shops everywhere.

THE *HIDDEN* GROSSNESS IN THE STUFF YOU BUY

The products below are just as gross as the items above, but their manufacturers would probably prefer that most people don't know how gross they really are.

PERFUME

Ambergris (AM-ber-grees) has been used for centuries as an ingredient in perfume to make the scent last longer. Although many perfume makers substitute artificial chemicals today, the best and most expensive perfumes still use the real thing. But ambergris is no sweet substance itself. Instead, it is a foul-smelling liquid concoction formed inside the stomach and intestines of a sperm whale, which the whale spits out in black chunks mixed with blood.

CLOTHING

A type of fabric, Harris tweed is still made today in Scotland the way it has been for hundreds of years—from yarn that is dyed with lichen (a combination of fungus and algae) that has been soaked in *human urine!*

71

TASTELESS TRIVIA: The use of perfume originated during the Bronze Age. An orange scent was worn by people to hide the odor of feces, as clothes were almost never changed and even more rarely washed.

IT'S A GAS

Natural gas, used for heating stoves and the like, has no odor. A gas leak, however, could be very dangerous, because a spark or flame in a room filled with gas could cause the room to explode. So the gas company adds an odor to the gas, a chemical called methyl mercaptan. This odor affects our sense of smell in such a vital way that the gas company has to add only the tiniest bit—*one billionth* of a gram to four hundred liters of gas—for us to sense it. Why does this chemical affect us in such a vital way? Because the scent comes from rotting animal flesh.

BARF BAGS

What is white, made of paper, open at one end, and measures $4\frac{1}{2}" \times 2\frac{5}{8}" \times 8\frac{1}{2}"$? A motion-sickness bag!

A familiar item to all who travel in airplanes, you can use them with confidence, because A.B. Specialty Packaging, the manufacturer of most of the motion-sickness bags used by airlines today, tests them by filling them with fluid to make sure they don't leak. Although they are also used for disposing used diapers and other soiled items, they are most commonly put to their original use. We can all fly a little easier knowing that should the need arise, we (or the person sitting next to us) will have a convenient, waterproof place to throw up.

72

THE BODY GROSS

People can be very creative. In some cases, you need look no further than their bodies to see this is true. You may be delighted by the extremes people have gone to in decorating the outside of their bodies. Or you may feel neutral. Certainly many of you, however, will be totally grossed out!

PIERCED PEOPLE

Pierced ears are nothing new; ever since Biblical times, people have had them. Pierced noses are less common, but an even newer fad is sweeping American and European cities. People are now piercing every part of their bodies—tongues, lips, nipples—any protruding body part is fair game, including the belly button.

MISCELLANEOUS MUTILATIONS

Lips: Members of the Sara tribe of central Africa insert flat wooden plates in the lips of their young women to make them larger. First they slit the lips and place a small disk inside. After some time has passed and the flesh has stretched, the plate is replaced with a larger one. This process is repeated until the upper lip protrudes four inches and the lower lip extends seven inches or more. Men of the Botocudo tribe in Brazil wear similar disks in their lips.

Teeth: In parts of Africa and Central America, teeth are filed or chipped into points. In Indonesia, the surfaces of the teeth are filed into a design.

Eyes: The Mayan Indians, until five hundred years ago, considered crossed eyes to be beautiful. They would hang a shiny ornament on their babies' foreheads, between the eyes, to cause this condition.

Neck: The women of the Padaung tribe of Burma wore brass rings around their necks, adding more rings as they grew to stretch their necks, sometimes to a height of fifteen inches.

Feet: The Chinese, from ancient times until as recently as the early 1900s, would tightly bind the feet of their young girls, deforming them in an attempt to achieve the perfect tiny foot.

FOUL FACT:

Up to five hundred years ago, Aztec and Mayan Indians forced a rope made of thorny vines through a hole in the tongue as a sacrifice.

73

HIDEOUS HISTORY

The history of human civilization has been a steady series of advances in science, art, and human understanding. Nevertheless, many a nauseating step has been taken to make these advances. Grab a barf bag and read on . . .

A BRIEF HISTORY OF GROSS

13TH CENTURY: TAP A VEIN

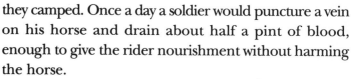

Marco Polo described how Mongol armies drank the blood of their horses so they could travel without food or having to light a fire when they camped. Once a day a soldier would puncture a vein on his horse and drain about half a pint of blood, enough to give the rider nourishment without harming the horse.

1348-1351: RING AROUND THE ROSIE

An epidemic of bubonic plague spread across Europe in the 14th century, wiping out a fourth of the population. The disease (which appears intermittently where there are unsanitary conditions) was carried by rats and transferred to people by fleas that bit the rats and also people. Two days after being bitten by an infected flea, a person's lymph glands became filled with pus. Veins burst under the skin, causing black spots to appear, which was where the name "the Black Death" came from. The bubonic fever seems to be the "inspiration" for this innocent childhood nursery rhyme:

Ring around the rosie,
A pocket full of posies,
Ashes, ashes,
We all fall down.

The "ring around the rosie" refers to the red-black spots on the body, the "pocket full of posies" was a charm used to ward off the disease, and the last line, "we all fall down," means we all drop dead.

1402: SKIN AND BONES

Following his death, Cardinal Lagrange of France had an unusually gross request in his will. He asked that his body be boned (which means having the bones removed) so that his skeleton could be buried at Avignon and his skin at Amiens. The two cities where he had divided his time during his life would divide his remains for eternity.

1557: PASS THE PRISONER

Hans Staden, a naval gunner from Germany, was fighting the Portuguese in Brazil when he was captured by the Tupinamba Indians. He described how prisoners of other tribes would be adopted by the Tupinamba, even allowed to marry their daughters, but then one day they would be killed and eaten by the Tupinamba. Even though these prisoners knew what was going to happen to them, they didn't try to escape. It was their fate, and they accepted it.

1753: STINKING SMUT OF WHEAT

A Frenchman named Tillet studied the smut fungus, which caused black, powdery spots to form on wheat. For hundreds of years, "smutty" bread was common and people had to tolerate the awful taste. Tillet developed a procedure that helped to stop the condition, but his cure may have been worse than the disease: the seeds of wheat were soaked in manure or putrefied urine.

18TH CENTURY: SHIPSHAPE

The British navy ruled the seas. However, conditions on board the ships were truly disgusting. They were rat-infested. The food was bad—meat was rotten, and butter so rancid that it had to be thrown overboard because it was stinking up the ship. Cheese was preserved by dipping it in tar, making it taste terrible. Flour was infested with weevils, and the bread and biscuits made from it were full of worms. Water, shipped in huge barrels, became "foul and odorous" and worm-infested, so a red-hot iron was thrown into the barrel in an attempt to make the water drinkable. Beer, stored in old oil and fish casks, was stinking and sour.

Tobias Smollett, a ship's doctor during this time, described the sick berth as more likely to kill people than help them get well. He wrote that the patients were kept far below decks, deprived of daylight and fresh air and breathing "nothing but the morbid steams exhaling from their own excrement and diseased bodies, devoured with vermin hatched in the filth that surrounded them."

1805: TAPPING THE ADMIRAL

Admiral Horatio Nelson died in the Battle of Trafalgar, and his body was shipped home to England for burial. As it was a long journey and the body needed to be preserved, it was placed in a barrel of brandy. When the barrel was opened in England, most of the brandy was gone. Apparently sailors, not knowing its contents, had tapped the barrel for drinks of brandy.

1822-1824: QUIT YER BELLYACHIN'

A musket accidentally fired, hitting Alexis St. Martin in the chest. In addition to other damage, it opened up his stomach. Surgeon William Beaumont arrived and found one of St. Martin's lungs and his stomach protruding from the wound. Beaumont poked them back in.

Surprising everyone, Alexis began to recover. Within three weeks he was much healthier and began eating. Unfortunately, everything he ate came out his still-open stomach wound. Dr. Beaumont wanted to close the wound, but Alexis, fearing surgery, refused. Instead, bandages were put over the wound. As long as a bandage was in place, Alexis ate and drank with no difficulty. But if the bandages were taken off, anything Alexis put in his mouth came out of the hole. Six months later the small hole was still there.

77

Dr. Beaumont realized that this wound would give him the chance to see the stomach in action. He took samples of the digestive juices from Alexis's stomach. He put food in small cotton bags, placed them in Alexis's stomach through the hole, then took them out hours later and weighed them to see how much had been dissolved. In order to sample the acidity of the gastric juices, Dr. Beaumont *tasted* them. This was a great stride forward in mankind's knowledge of how the stomach worked, as well as a highlight in gross history.

1878: GIVE HIM THE HOOK

Three Italian researchers, G. B. Grasi, C. Parona, and E. Parona, discovered eggs in the feces of people infested with hookworms. They could not, however, determine how the infestation was passed on to the next victim, so one of the researchers volunteered to swallow some of the feces. Although it was filled with eggs, he was not infested with hookworms. (Later researchers discovered that the worms can only infest someone if they enter the body *after* they hatch.)

1907: TYPHOID MARY

Typhoid Mary, a carrier of typhoid who displayed no symptoms of her own, was quarantined in 1907 after spreading the disease to hundreds of people in New York City by handling food with soiled hands. Typhoid fever, a bacterial infection, is caused by eating food or drinking water that has been contaminated with excrement from someone who has the disease. Released in 1910, Mary returned to her old tricks in 1914, when she was caught again and spent the remainder of her life in quarantine.

1966: HAVING A BABY

A new method was developed to help infertile women become pregnant: they were given an extract from the pituitary gland. Unfortunately, there were only two sources for the extract: mortuaries would supply the pituitary glands of ten dead women, or older women would provide a month's worth of urine, which doctors would concentrate before removing the extract.

1992: LOSING FACE

In January, President George Bush was at a state dinner in Tokyo, Japan. The President was not feeling well. In between the raw salmon with caviar and the grilled beef with pepper sauce, he pushed back his chair, opened his mouth, and spewed the contents of his stomach all over the pants of the Prime Minister of Japan.

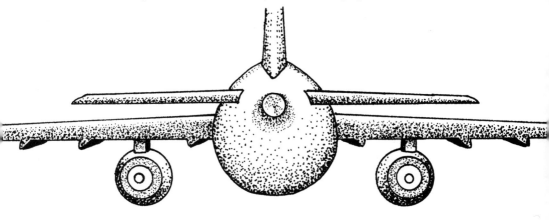

1992: LOOK TO THE SKIES

On October 18, a glob of green ice crashed through the roof of the Cinnamon family's living room. A ball of frozen disinfectant and human waste had fallen from the belly of a passing airliner. Gerri Cinnamon had to store the material in her freezer until the insurance company and the Federal Aviation Administration arrived to investigate.

79

IN CONCLUSION

There's no doubt about it, it's a gross world after all—if, that is, you know where to look. Under your bed, in your refrigerator, or crashing through your living room ceiling, something gross is just waiting to be discovered by, or happen to, you!

Index